Pocket CANTONESE

Dictionary

Compiled by
Philip Yungkin Lee

PERIPLUS

Published by Periplus Editions (HK) Ltd.
Copyright © 2003 Periplus Editions

ISBN: 0-7946-0143-X

Printed in Singapore

Distributed by:

Asia-Pacific
Berkeley Books Pte Ltd
130 Joo Seng Road, 06-01/03
Singapore 368357
Tel: (65) 6280 1330
Fax: (65) 6280 6290
Email: inquiries@periplus.com.sg

Japan
Tuttle Publishing
Yaekari Building, 3F
5-4-12 Osaki, Shinagawa-ku
Tokyo 1530064, Japan
Tel: (03) 5437 0171
Fax: (03) 5437 0755
Email: tuttle-sales@gol.com

North America, Latin America & Europe
Tuttle Publishing
364 Innovation Drive
North Clarendon, VT 05759-9436, USA
Tel: (802) 773 8930
Fax: (802) 773 8993
Email: info@tuttlepublishing.com
www.periplus.com

08 07 06 05 04
8 7 6 5 4 3 2

Contents

Introduction

This Pocket Dictionary is an indispensable companion for visitors to Hong Kong, Macau, or the province of Guangdong in southern China, and for anyone in the early stages of learning the language spoken by most overseas Chinese. It contains all the 3,000 or so Cantonese words that are most commonly encountered in colloquial, everyday speech.

For the sake of clarity, only the common Cantonese equivalents for each English word have been given. When an English word has more than one possible meaning, with different Cantonese equivalents, each meaning is listed separately, with a clear explanatory gloss. The layout is clear and accessible, with none of the abbreviations and dense nests of entries typical of many small dictionaries.

The language represented in this dictionary is spoken as an everyday language by over 50 million people in China and by substantial minority communities in Malaysia, Vietnam, and Singapore. It is primarily an oral language, but may be written in the same script as other Chinese languages, including Modern Standard Chinese ('Mandarin' or 'Putongua').

Speakers of all Chinese languages are able to read and understand the same script, because it does not relate directly to the sounds of the language. Instead it makes use of a very large number of characters representing different syllables, to each of which is linked both a meaning and a sound. The meaning attached to each character is the same for each of the Chinese languages and dialects, although the way it is pronounced may well be different. In this way, writing can serve as a means of communication between Chinese from geographically separated regions who would not be able to understand each other's speech.

Since the 1950s the government of the People's Republic of China has promoted the simplification of a number of characters that are complex in formation or contain a large number of strokes, but these reforms have not generally been adopted in Hong Kong. All the Cantonese words and phrases in this dictionary are written using the traditional forms of characters, although the simplified forms are also readily understood.

Many Cantonese words and particles cannot be represented by conventional Chinese characters. A number of special characters have been invented for use in writing Cantonese, and this process continues wherever the language is used as a means of written expression, such as in the comic books produced in Hong Kong.

In this dictionary every Cantonese word or phrase is also given in the roman alphabet, following the 'Yale' system which is the most widely used system in language books and dictionaries. A guide to the pronunciation of these romanized forms is given on the following pages.

Chinese is a tonal language, and Cantonese has even more tones than Mandarin. It is extremely important to use the correct tone in pronouncing each syllable. In this dictionary the tones are indicated by diacritical marks over the vowels.

The words and phrase in the Cantonese-English section of the dictionary are arranged in English alphabetical order using the letters and diacritical marks of the romanized forms. Words that have the same spelling but different tones are listed in the order first, second, third, fourth, fifth and sixth tone. Secondly, in the case of characters represented by the same roman letters which also have the same tone, alphabetization follows the principle that simpler characters (those composed of fewer strokes) are listed before more complex characters (those composed of more strokes). Examples of this are given on the following pages.

Although the writing system and pronunciation of Cantonese may be daunting for English speakers, grammatically it's not too problematic. There are no inflections as such (distinctions such as tense and number being indicated by various particles) and the word order is generally the same as in English.

Pronunciation

The Yale system of romanization

The system used in this dictionary to write Cantonese with roman letters is the *Yale* system which is the most widely used system in language books and dictionaries. The imitated pronunciation should be read as if it were English, bearing in mind the following main points:

Consonants

b, ch, d, f, g, h, j, k, l, m, n, p, s, t, w, y as in English.

ng	like English **ng** in si**ng**
gw	as in the English name **Gw**endolyn
kw	like English **Gw**endolyn with a strong puff of air

Vowels

a	like English **u** in 'b**u**rr'
a(a)	like English **a** in 'f**a**thers. This long vowel is normally written **aa**. However, it is written **a** when it is used by itself without a consonant ending (except **h** which is used as a tone indicator for the 4th, 5th and 6th tones).
e	like English **e** in 't**e**n'
i	like English **ee** in 'f**ee**'
o	like English **o** in 'h**o**t'
u	like English **oo** in 'f**oo**l'
eu	like English **e** in 'h**e**r' with rounded lips
yu	like French **ü**. In English is pronounced like 'j**ee**p' with lips rounded and pushed out.

Tones

A tone is a variation in pitch by which a syllable can be pronounced. In Cantonese, a variation of pitch or tone changes the meaning of the word. There are six tones: the 1st tone is indicated by a horizontal tone mark; the 2nd tone is indicated by a rising tone mark; the 3rd tone does not carry a tone mark; the 4th tone is indicated by a falling tone mark along with the letter 'h' placed at the end of the vowel or group of vowels; the 5th tone is indicated by a rising tone mark along with the letter 'h' placed at the end of the vowel or group of vowels; the 6th tone is indicated by the letter 'h' placed at the end of the vowel or group of vowels. Like the 3rd tone, it does not carry a tone mark. Tone marks are placed on the first vowel of a group of vowels. Below is a tone chart which describes tones using the 5-degree notation. It divides the range of pitches from lowest (1) to highest (5).

Tone chart

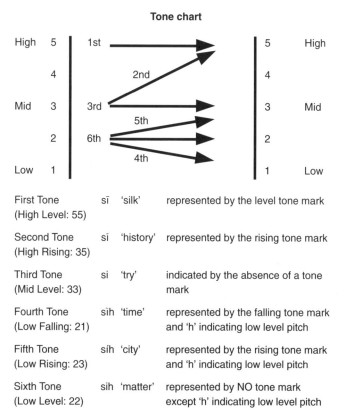

First Tone (High Level: 55)	sī	'silk'	represented by the level tone mark
Second Tone (High Rising: 35)	sí	'history'	represented by the rising tone mark
Third Tone (Mid Level: 33)	si	'try'	indicated by the absence of a tone mark
Fourth Tone (Low Falling: 21)	sìh	'time'	represented by the falling tone mark and 'h' indicating low level pitch
Fifth Tone (Low Rising: 23)	síh	'city'	represented by the rising tone mark and 'h' indicating low level pitch
Sixth Tone (Low Level: 22)	sih	'matter'	represented by NO tone mark except 'h' indicating low level pitch

Conventions used in this dictionary

1. Syllables are joined together to form words. The joining of syllables is called juncture and this process helps you to look at sounds as an integral unit rather than disjoined syllables. Where juncture creates confusion as to where one syllable ends and the next syllable begins, an apostrophe is used to indicate that juncture exists, e.g. wíhng'yúhn 'forever'.

2. For a syllable containing a diphthong or a triphthong, the tone mark always falls on the first written vowel, e.g. kéuih 'he/she', háau 'test', covering the tone value of the whole syllable. In the syllables m̀h 'not' and ńgh 'five' which have no vowel letters, the tone mark is written over the consonants m̀ and ǵ respectively.

3. An asterisk written next to a syllable indicates a changed tone, e.g. Gwóngdūng-wá* Cantonese, Yīngmán* 'English' etc.

4. The hyphen is used to indicate:
   (a) numbers above ten, e.g. sahp-yāt 'twelve', gáu-sahp-gáu 'ninety-nine',

(b)   verb-object constructions, e.g. cheung-gō 'sing'

(c)   verb with special markers, e.g. làih-jó 'came', làih-gán 'coming'

(d)   compound nouns modified by adjectives, e.g. Méihgwok-yàhn 'American/s';

(e)   comparative adjectives, e.g. chìh-dī 'later'

(f)   days of the week, months, e.g. Sīngkèih-yaht 'Sunday', Sahp-yuht 'October'

(g)   reduplicated forms of nouns and adjectives, e.g. chī-lahp-lahp 'sticky'.

(h)   adverbs ending in -ly, e.g. póupin-gám* 'generally'

Alphabetical ordering

The words and phrases collected in the Cantonese-English glossary are arranged alphabetically using the Yale system of romanization. In this system each syllable (represented by a character) is a unit. The first character in a word or phrase is the head character. Each word or phrase is ordered in the first instance according to the phonetic value of this character. In a succession of entries having the same head character, alphabetical order is then determined by the phonetic value of the second character. This arrangement has the advantage of enhancing meaning by grouping together words which share a common character 'root', even though it is done at the expense of a straight alphabetical ordering.

The ordering of characters is affected by two other considerations. Firstly, in the case of characters represented by the same roman letters, alphabetization is determined by the tone of each character (represented in Yale romanization by diacritics and the use of the letter 'h' placed after the end of a vowel or group of vowels), in the order first, second, third, fourth, fifth and sixth tone. Secondly, in the case of characters represented by the same roman letters which also have the same tone, alphabetization follows the principle that simpler characters (those composed of fewer strokes) are listed before more complex characters (those composed of more strokes).

It is uncommon that a Cantonese syllable carries the full range of six tones, but it is useful to use such examples to illustrate the alphabetical order based on tone sequence. For example, the 268th - 294th entries under S have as their head character variations of the syllable 'si'. These entries are sī - first tone (2 instances of a 7-stroke character), (1 of a 9-stroke character), (2 of a 12-stroke character), and (1 of a 15-stroke character); sí - second tone (1 instance); si - third tone which does not carry a diacritic (5 instances of the same character), sìh - fourth tone which combines the falling diacritic with the letter 'h' (4 instances of the same character); síh - fifth tone which combines the rising diacritic with the letter 'h' (4 instances of the same character); and sih - sixth tone which does not carry a diacritic but has the letter 'h' after the vowel of the syllable (1 instance of a 3-stroke character), (5 instances of a 8-stroke character) and (1 instance of another 8-stroke character).

Cantonese–English

A

a'bā /a'bàh 呀爸 father
a'màh 呀嫲 grandmother (paternal)
ayèh 呀爺 grandfather (paternal)
Ajāu 亞洲 Asia
àh 牙 tooth, teeth
àh'cháat* 牙刷 toothbrush
àh'gōu 牙膏 toothpaste
aai(gāau) 嗌（交） to argue
aak'lihk 壓力 pressure
aahk'ngoih/oih ge 額外嘅 extra
aahk'tàuh 額頭 forehead
āam 啱 correct
āam'sān 啱身 fitting, suitable
āam'āam 啱啱 just now
àahm'duhng 岩洞 cave
aan 晏 late at night
aan'jau 晏晝 midday
àahn'sīk 顏色 color
áahn 眼 eye
áahnfan 眼瞓 sleepy
áahn'gēng* 眼鏡 eyeglasses, spectacles
áahn'leuih 眼淚 tears
áahn'mèih 眼眉 eyebrow
áahn'mèih-mòuh 眼眉毛 eyelashes
aahng 硬 hard, stiff
aahng'pùhn 硬盤 hard disk/drive (computer)
aahng'jí-bán 硬纸板 cardboard
aap 鴨 duck
áau'tyúhn 拗斷 to break apart
áauh 咬 to bite
ái 矮 short (not tall)

ái'gwā 矮瓜 eggplant, aubergine
àih'hím 危險 danger, dangerous
aih'seuht 藝術 art
aih'seuht-gā 藝術家 artist
āk(yàhn) 呃（人） to cheat
am 暗 dark
àhn 銀 silver
àhn'bāau 銀包 wallet, purse
àhn'jí 銀纸 note (currency)
àhn'hòhng 銀行 bank (finance)
áu 嘔 to vomit
āu'jāu 歐洲 Europe
áuh'yìhn 偶然 by chance
áuh'yìhn-gāan 偶然間 occasionally
àuh'náaih/láaih 牛奶 milk
àuh'yuhk 牛肉 beef
àuh'ná/lá 牛嫲 cow
àuh'yàuh 牛油 butter

B

bāsí 巴士 bus
bāsí-jaahm 巴士站 bus stop
bàhbā* 爸爸 father
bah-gūng 罷工 to go on strike
báai-tói 擺檯 to lay the table
báai'tyut 擺脫 get rid of
baak 百 hundred
baakfahn-léut* 百分率 percentage
baakfahnjī-.... 百分之- ... percent
baakfo-gūngsī 百貨公司 department store
baak-maahn 百萬 million
baak 伯 uncle (father's older brother)

B

baak'nèuhng/lèuhng 伯娘 aunt (wife of father's older brother)

baahkchoi 白菜 cabbage, Chinese

baahkfaahn 白飯 rice (cooked)

baahksīk 白色 white

bāandím ge 斑點嘅 spotted (pattern)

bāan'gēi 班機 flight

bāan'gēi-houhmáh 班機號碼 flight number

baahn'gūng-sāt 辦公室 office

baat 八 eight

baat-sahp 八十 eighty

Baat-yuht 八月 August

bāau 包 to wrap

bāaugwó 包裹 parcel, package

bāaujōng 包裝 to package

bāau'kwut 包括 included, including

báau 飽 full, eaten one's fill

bākbihn 北邊 north

Bākgīng 北京 Beijing

Bākhòhn 北韓 Korea, North

bān'gwún 賓館 guesthouse

bahn 笨 stupid

bāng 泵 pump

bāngdáai* 繃帶 bandage

bātdaahn ... yìhché 不但 ... 而且 not only ... but also

bātdouhdāk 不道德 wrong (morally)

bātgwo 不過 nevertheless

bātleih tiuhgín* 不利條件 handicap

bātgei-bóu 筆記簿 notebook

bēi'ngōi/ōi 悲哀 sorrow

beimaht 秘密 secret

beisyū 秘書 secretary

bēi 比 than

bēichoi 比賽 match, competition

bēigaau 比較 rather, fairly

bēi 俾 let, to give, to allow

bēi yàhn tái 俾人睇 to show

bēi ... yigin 俾 ... 意見 to advise

bēi-chín* 俾錢 to pay

beih màihwaahk 被迷惑 puzzled

beihgō 鼻哥 nose

beihgō-lūng 鼻哥窿 nostril

beihyahn 避孕 contraceptive

beihyahn-tou 避孕套 condom

beihyahn-yún 避孕丸 contraceptive pill

beng 柄 handle

behng 病 to be sick, illness

behngyàhn 病人 patient (doctor's)

bénggōn 餅乾 biscuit

bìhbī BB baby

bìhbī-chòhng BB 床 cot

bīk 逼 crowded

bīk(yàhn) 逼 (人) busy (crowded)

binhóu-jó 變好咗 to get better (improve)

bīndouh 邊度 where

bīndouh dōu mh'hái 邊度都唔喺 nowhere

bīn'gaai 邊界 border (between countries)

bīn'go 邊個 who, which

bīn júng 邊 (種) what kind of

bīnsyu 邊處 where

bīn wái* 邊位 who

bīnyùhn 邊緣 border, edge

bihnbei 便秘 constipation

bihnwuh 辯護 defend (with words)

bīng 冰 ice

bīngdung 冰凍 frozen

bītsēui 必需 necessary

bīu 表 meter (in taxi)

bīu 錶 watch (wristwatch)

bīujéun 標準 level (standard)

bīuji 標誌 sign, symbol

bīutàih 標題 title (of book, film)

bīugaak 表格 form (to fill out)

bīumihn 表面 surface

bīusih 表示 express, state

bīuyihn 表現 to behave

bīuyín 表演 show (live performance)

C

bō 波 ball
bōlohng 波浪 wave (in sea)
bōlēi 玻璃 glass (material)
bōlēi-būi 玻璃杯 glass (for drinking)
bōchoi 菠菜 spinach
bōlō 菠蘿 pineapple
bo-yām 播音 to broadcast
bokmaht-gwún 博物館 museum
boktàuh 膊頭 shoulder
bohkmouh 薄霧 mist
bōng 幫 to help
bōngjoh 幫助 to assist, assistance
bōngmòhng 幫忙 to assist
bóng 綁 to tie
bohng 磅 to weigh
bóu'chyùhn 保存 to save, to keep
bóuhím 保險 insurance
bóujing 保証 guarantee
bóulàuh 保留 to keep, to preserve
bóumaht 保密 to keep a secret
bóuwaih 保衛 defend (in war)
bóuwuh 保護 to guard
bóuwuh-kēui 保護區 reserve (for animals)
bóuléuih 堡壘 fortress
bou 布 cloth
bouliú* 布料 fabric, textile
boulām 布冧 plum
boují 報紙 newspaper
bougou 報告 report
bouh 步 step
bouhfahn 部分 part (not whole)
bouhlohk 部落 tribe
bouhmùhn 部門 department
buhkbou 瀑布 waterfall
buhnléuih 伴侶 partner (spouse)
būi 杯 cup
būi'gwaih 杯櫃 cupboard
buijek 背脊 back (part of body)
buijek-gwāt 背脊骨 spine
buisām 背心 vest, undershirt

būn 搬 move from one place to another
būn'ngūk/ūk 搬屋 to move (house)
bunsāangsuhk 半生熟 rare (uncooked)
bunyeh 半夜 midnight

C

chā 叉 fork
chāyih 差異 difference (in quality)
chābiht 差別 difference (discrepancy in figures)
chàh 茶 tea
chàh 查 look up (find in book)
chàahnyán 殘忍 cruel
cháai-dāanchē 踩單車 to ride (bicycle)
cháak*/chaahk 賊 thief
chāakyihm 測驗 to test
chāamgā 參加 to participate, to attend
chāamgwūn 參觀 visit
chāamyúh 參與 to go along, to join in
chāan 餐 meal
cháang 橙 orange, citrus
cháang-gām-leuih 橙柑類 citrus
cháangsīk 橙色 orange (color)
chāan'gwūn 餐館 restaurant
chaap'táu*/tàuh 插頭 socket (electric)
chaat 刷 to brush
cháat* 刷 brush
chaat-gōnjehng 擦乾淨 to scrub
chaat-gwōng 擦光 to polish
cháatjí-gāau 擦紙料 rubber (eraser)
chāau 抄 to copy
cháau (kéuih) yàuhyú* 炒(佢) 魷魚 to fire someone
chai-màaih yātchàih 砌埋一齊 to assemble, to put together

- chānchìk 親戚 relatives, family
- chān'ngáahn/áahn gin-dóu* 親眼見到 to witness
- chàhmkàuh 尋求 to seek
- chàhmmáahn 尋晚 last night
- chàhnliht 陳列 display, to display
- chàhn'gauu 陳舊 worn out (clothes, machine)
- chàhng 層 layer
- chàhng/láu* 層／樓 story (of a building)
- chàhnggīng 曾經 ever, have already
- chāt 七 seven
- chāt-sahp 七十 seventy
- Chāt-yuht 七月 July
- chāutīn 秋天 autumn, fall (season)
- chauhei 臭氣 odor, bad smell
- chaumeih 臭味 smell, bad odor
- cháuyēung* 醜樣 ugly
- chàuhbaahn 籌辦 to arrange
- chē 車 vehicle, automobile
- chēdouh 車道 lane (of a highway)
- chēfòhng 車房 garage (for parking)
- chēlūk 車碌 wheel
- chēsin 車線 lane (of a highway)
- chekchyun 尺寸 measurements
- chēng-nìhng/lìhng'mūng 青檸檬 lime, citrus
- chēngdáu* 青豆 peas
- chéng 請 invite
- chéngmahn 請問 excuse me! (attracting attention)
- chēui-gōn 吹乾 to dry
- chēui 催 to urge, to push for
- chēui-wái 催毀 destroyed, ruined
- chéuisiu 取笑 to laugh at
- chéuisīu 取消 cancel
- chèuih 除 divided by
- chèuihfēi 除非 unless
- chèuih-jó ... jī'ngoih/oih 除咗 ... 之外 apart from, besides

- chèuih-sāam 除衫 to get undressed
- chèuihfòng* 廚房 kitchen
- chèuihsī 廚師 cook (person)
- chēuntīn 春天 spring (season)
- chéun 蠢 stupid
- chēung 窗 window (in house)
- chēungháu 窗口 window (for paying, buying tickets)
- chēunglím* 窗簾 curtain
- chēunggau 搶救 to rescue
- cheung-gō 唱歌 to sing
- chèuhng 長 long (size)
- chèuhngbeng-chìhgāng 長柄匙羹 ladle, dipper
- chèuhngdēk* 長笛 flute
- chèuhngdouh 長度 length
- chèuhngfōng-yìhng 長方形 rectangle
- chèuhnglùhng 長龍 queue, line
- chèuhng 牆 wall
- chēut-jó-heui 出咗去 out
- chēutbáan 出版 to publish
- chēutfaat 出發 departure
- chēut-gāai hàhng-háh 出街行吓 to go for a walk
- chēut'háu 出口 exit, export, to export
- chēut-heui 出去 to go out, exit
- chēut-hohn 出汗 to sweat
- chēut-jó-gāai 出咗街 out
- chēutmèng* 出名 famous
- chēut'nín*/lín* 出年 next year
- chēut'sai 出世 to be born
- chēutsāng yahtkèih 出生日期 date of birth
- chēut'sauh 出售 sale, for
- chēut'yihn 出現 appear, become visible
- chī-nahp/lahp-nahp/lahp 黐笠笠 sticky
- chí'ngoih/oih 此外 in addition
- chijeuih 次序 sequence, order
- chiyiu ge 次要嘅 minor (not important)
- chisau 刺繡 embroidery
- chisó 廁所 toilet

chìhfùh 似乎 to seem

chìh 詞 word

chìhdín 詞典 dictionary

chìhdíp* 磁碟 diskette

chìhdou 遲到 late (for an appointment)

chìhgāng 匙羹 spoon

chīmjing 簽証 visa

chīm-méng* 簽名 signature, to sign

chīn 千 thousand

chīn-maahn 千萬 ten million

chín 淺 shallow

chín* 錢 money

chìhnbaih 錢幣 currency

chìhnjeun 前進 advance, go forward

chìhnmihn 前面 front

chìhnyaht 前日 day before yesterday

chīngchēun 青春 youth (state of being young)

chīng-siu'nìhn/lìhn 青少年 teenager

chīngdaahm 清淡 mild (not spicy)

chīngtōng 清湯 soup (clear)

chīngjaan 稱贊 praise

chíng 請 please go ahead

chíngkàuh 請求 to request (informally)

chíngmahn 請問 excuse me! (attracting attention)

ching 秤 to weigh, scales

chìhngdouh 程度 degree, level

chìhngfong 情況 situation, how things are

chìhngléih jī'noih/loih 情理之內 within reason

chìhnglóhng 晴朗 sunny

chìhngséuih 情緒 emotion

chìhngyihn 呈現 to reveal (make visible)

chit 切 to cut

chitdái 徹底 completely

chīuchēut 超出 to go beyond

chìuhsāp 潮濕 humid, damp

Chìuhsīn 朝鮮 North Korea

Chìuhsīn-yàhn 朝鮮人 Korean (North)

Chìuhsīn-mán*'màhn 朝鮮文 Korean (language)

Chìuhsīn-yúh 朝鮮語 Korean (language)

chīukāp-sìhchèuhng 超級市場 supermarket

cho 錯 wrong (mistaken)

cho'ngh 錯誤 error, mistake

chóh 坐 sit, to

chóh-fóchē 坐火車 by rail

chóhchē 坐車 to ride(transport)

chóh-dāi 坐低 sit down, to

chóipiu 彩票 lottery

choidāan 菜單 menu

chòihcháan 財產 property

chòihmaht 財物 belongings

chòihlíu* 材料 material, ingredient

chongjok 創作 to create

chongjouh 創造 to create

chòhng 床 bed

chòhngdāan 床單 bedsheet

chòhngyúk* 床褥 mattress

chōujok-haihtúng 操作系統 operating system (computer)

chōulóuh 粗魯 rough

chóu 草 grass

chou 醋 vinegar

chòuh 嘈 noisy

chùhng 從 from

chùhng 蟲 insect

chùhngfūk 重複 to repeat

chùhnglàhm 叢林 jungle

chúhng 重 heavy

chúhngleuhng 重量 weight

chūkdouh 速度 speed

chūng-fāsá 冲花洒 to take a shower

chūnglèuhng 冲涼 to bathe, to take a bath

chūnglèuhng-fóng* 冲涼房 bathroom

chūnglohng 冲浪 surf

chūngsái 冲洗 to develop (film)

- chūngséui 沖水 flush (wash)
- chūngmìhng 聰明 clever, smart, wise
- chúngmaht 寵物 pet animal
- chyúléih 處理 to handle
- chyùhfóng* 廚房 kitchen
- chyùhsī 廚師 cook (person)
- chyúh 柱 post, column
- chyúhchòhng 儲藏 to store
- chyūn 穿 to pierce, to penetrate
- chyūnjōng 村莊 village
- chyun 串 to spell
- chyunsīu 串燒 skewer
- chyùhnbouh 全部 entirety, whole
- chyùhn'gíng 全景 panorama
- chyùhn'gwok-sing 全國性 national
- chyùhnfong 存放 deposit (leave behind with someone)
- chyùhnfún 存款 deposit (put money in the bank)
- chyùhnjoih 存在 to exist
- chyùhnsām 存心 intention
- chyùhnjān 傳真 fax
- chyùhn'syut 傳說 legend
- chyùhntúng 傳統 traditional
- chyùhnyíhm 傳染 contagious

D

- dá 打 to strike, to hit
- dá-dihnwá* 打電話 to ring (on the telephone)
- dá-baaih 打敗 beat (to defeat)
- dá-gāau 打交 to fight (physically)
- dágáau 打擾 to disturb
- dáhfóh-gēi 打火機 lighter
- dá-fòhngyihk-jām 打防疫針 vaccination
- dá-fūng 打風 storm, typhoon
- dá-láahngjan 打冷震 to shiver
- dá-haamlouh 打喊路 yawn
- dá-hātchī 打乞嚏 to sneeze
- dá-hōi 打開 to open
- dá-jām 打針 injection
- dá-jeung 打仗 to make war
- dá-jih 打字 to type
- dá-laahn 打爛 break, shatter
- dá-lèuih 打雷 thunder
- dásyun 打算 to plan
- dáyan 打印 to print (from computer)
- daai 帶 to carry
- daaih 大 big, large
- daaih-gáamga 大減價 sale (reduced prices)
- daaihbaak 大伯 brother-in-law (husband's older brother)
- daaihbahnjeuhng 大笨象 elephant
- daaihbihn 大便 to defecate
- daaih-bouhfahn 大部分 mostly
- daaihhah 大廈 building
- daaihhohk 大學 university
- daaihji seuhng 大致上 on the whole
- daaih-jihyìhn 大自然 nature
- daaihkáuh 大舅 brother-in-law (wife's older brother)
- daaih'kói*/koi 大概 more or less
- daaihlāu 大樓 coat, overcoat
- daaihlóu 大佬 brother (older)
- daaihluhk 大陸 mainland (often refer to China)
- daaihmùhn 大門 gate
- daaihsēng 大聲 loud
- daaihsēng ngaai/aai 大聲嗌 to shout
- daaihsēng giu 大聲叫 to cry out, to yell
- daaihsíh 大使 ambassador
- daaihsíh-gwún 大使館 embassy
- daaihsai 大細 measurements
- daaihtàuh-jām 大頭針 pin
- daaihtéui 大腿 thigh
- daaih'yéuk*/yeuk 大約 roughly, approximately
- dāambóu 担保 to guarantee
- dāamsām 擔心 to worry

dāam'ngh 耽誤 to delay
dāan 單 bill
dāanchē 單車 bicycle
dāanchīhng-piu 單程票 one-way ticket
dāandiuh 單調 bland
dāanduhk 單獨 alone
dāansān 單身 single (not married)
dāanwái* 單位 flat, apartment
daahnhaih 但係 but, however
daahn'gōu 蛋糕 cake, pastry
daahn'gūng 彈弓 spring (metal part)
daap 答 to answer (spoken)
daapying 答應 to promise
daap-seuhnfūng-chē 搭順風車 lift (ride in car)
daahtdou 達到 to reach, to get to
dahkbiht 特別 special
dahkdím 特點 characteristic
dahkyìhn 突然 suddenly
dāi 低 low
dái 底 bottom (base)
dáifu 底褲 underpants
dáisāam 底衫 undershirt
dàihdái* 弟弟 brother (younger)
daihfúh 弟婦 sister-in-law (wife of husband's younger brother)
daihsāam 第三 third (in a series)
daihyih 第二 second (in sequence)
daihyih dī 第二啲 else: anything else
daihyih go 第二個 another (different)
daihsung 遞送 to deliver
dāk 得 fine (okay)
dāk-dóu* 得到 to get, to receive
dākjeuih 得罪 offend
dākjéung-yàhn 得獎人 winner
dākyi 得意 interesting (action)
Dakgwok 德國 Germany

Dākgwok ge 德國嘅 German (in general)
Dākgwok-yàhn 德國人 German (people)
Dāk'mán*/màhn 德文 German (language)
dám 揼 to throw
dāng 燈 light (lamp)
dāng-séuhng 登上 to go up, to climb
dáng 等 to wait for
dáng yātjahn 等一陣 moment (in a moment)
dang 凳 stool, chair
dáufān 糾紛 dispute
dauhfuh 豆腐 beancurd, tofu
dauhsih 豆豉 black beans
dehngdāan 訂單 order (placed for goods)
deih 地 land
deihfōng 地方 place, space
deihjan 地震 earthquake
deihjí 地址 address
deihjīn 地氈 carpet
deihkàuh 地球 Earth, the world
deihkēui 地區 area, region
deihmihn 地面 ground, earth
deihtòuh 地圖 map
deihwaih 地位 rank, station in life
dēng 釘 nail (spike)
déng* 頂 top
dehng 訂 order (placed for goods)
dēui*/deuih 隊 team
deui (yàhn) 對（人） to treat (behave towards), toward
deui ... jau-mèihtàuh 對 ... 皺眉頭 frown
deuifuh 對付 to deal with
deuigok 對角 diagonally
deuigok-sin 對角線 diagonal
deuilaahp ge 對立嘅 opposed, in opposition
deui'mh'jyuh 對唔住 sorry!
deuimihn 對面 opposite (facing)

D

deuisáu 對手 rival, opponent

deuiwuhn 兌換 to exchange (money, opinions)

deuiwuhn-léut* 兌換率 exchange rate

deuiyihn 兌現 to cash a check

dīkkok 的確 quite (very)

dīksí 的士 taxi

dihkyàhn 敵人 enemy

dím-choi 點菜 order (placed for food)

dím(yēung*) 點 (樣) how?

dím(jūng) 點 (鐘) o'clock

dímgáai 點解 why? what for

dīn 顛 insane

dínláih 典禮 ceremony

dínyìhng# 典型 typical

dihndāanchē 電單車 motorcycle

dihnduhng ge 電動嘅 electric

dihnduhng-làuhtāi 電動樓梯 escalator

dihnhei-yuhngbán 電器用品 appliance, electrical

dihnjí 電子 electronic

dihnjí-yàuhgín* 電子郵件 email (message)

dihnjí-yàuhgín* deihjí 電子郵件地址 email address

dihnlàuh 電流 electricity

dihnsih 電視 television

dihnsih-gēi 電視機 TV

dihntāi 電梯 lift, elevator

dihntúng 電筒 flashlight, torch

dihnwá* 電話 telephone

dihnwá* houhmáh 電話號碼 telephone number

dihnwá* làuhyìhn 電話留言 voicemail

dihnyàuh 電油 petrol, gasoline

dihnyàuh-jaahm 電油站 gasoline station

dihnyíng 電影 film, movie

dihn'nóuh/lóuh 電腦 computer

(gwōng)díp* (光) 碟 compact disc

dihp 碟 dish, platter

dit-dóu 跌倒 fall over

dit-lohklàih 跌落嚟 fall, to

dihtjeuih 秩序 orderly

diuhtàuh 掉頭 to reverse (a vehicle), to back up

dīusok 雕塑 sculpture

diu-yū* 釣魚 to fish

dō 多 much, many

dō-dī 多啲 more (comparative)

dōwàhn 多雲 cloudy, overcast

dōyùh ge 多餘嘅 unnecessary

dói* 袋 bag, pocket

doihtai 代替 to replace

dōjeh 多謝 thank you (money, gifts)

dōng 當 when, at the time

dōngjūng 當中 middle: be in the middle of doing

dōngyìhn 當然 of course

dōngyìhn hóyíh 當然可以 certainly!

dōu 刀 knife

dōuhaih 都係 as well, also

dōu 島 island

dóu 倒 to pour

dóumùih 倒霉 unlucky

dou'jyun 倒轉 upside down

dóubok 賭博 gamble

dou 到 to arrive

dou'chyu 到處 everywhere

doudaaht 到達 arrival

douh'geih 妒忌 jealous, jealousy

douh 度 degrees (temperature)

douhbiht 道別 say goodbye

Douhgaau 道教 Taoism

douhhip 道歉 to apologize

douhjeh 道謝 say thank you

douhsyùhn 渡船 ferry

douhtìhn 稻田 rice fields

douhyàuh 導遊 lead (tour guide)

duhkbán 毒品 drug (recreational)

duhkyeuhk 毒藥 poison

dūngbāk 東北 north-east

dūng'bīn/bihn 東邊 east

F

dūng'nàahm/làahm 東南 south-east

dūngtīn 冬天 winter

dúngsih-jéung 董事長 director (of company)

duhngjok 動作 movement, motion

duhngmaht 動物 animal

duhngmaht-yùhn 動物園 zoo

dyún 短 short (concise)

dyúnfu 短褲 shorts (short trousers)

dyúnjaahm 短暫 short time, a moment

dyúnjaahm ge 短暫嘅 brief

F

fā 花 flower

fāpìhng 花瓶 vase

fāsá 花洒 shower (for washing)

fāsāng 花生 peanut

fāyún 花園 garden, yard

fajōng-bán 化妝品 cosmetics

fàahn 煩 bother, disturbance

faahn 瓣 cloves

faai 快 fast, rapid, quick

faai-dī 快啲 faster

faai-dī lā 快啲啦！ come on, let's go, hurry up!

faai-dī hóu-fāan 快啲好番 get well soon!

faaijí 筷子 chopsticks

fāan-heui 返去 to go back

fāan-jyuntàuh 返轉頭 to return, to go back

fāan-làih 返嚟 to come back

fāan-ngūk/ūk'kéi* 返屋企 to go home

fāan'gáan 番碱 soap

fāankē 番茄 tomato

fāan-jó 翻咗 overturned

fāan-gwoheui 翻過去 to turn over

fāanyihk 翻譯 to translate, interpreter

fáandeui 反對 to object, to protest

fáanyíng 反映 to reflect

fáanying 反應 to respond, to react

faat-baahkyaht-muhng 發白日夢 to daydream

faatchau 發臭 to stink

faat-chyùhnjān 發傳真 to fax

faat-dihnjí-yàuhgín* 發電子郵件 email, to

faatduhng 發動 to start

faatgwōng ge 發光嘅 shiny

faatjín 發展 development, to develop

faatmìhng 發明 to invent

faatmuhng 發夢 to dream

faat'nāu/lāu 發嬲 to get angry

faatsāng 發生 to happen, to occur

faatsāng mātyéh sih 發生乜嘢事 happened, what happened?

faatsīu 發燒 fever

faatyām 發音 to pronounce

faatyihn 發現 to discover

Faatgwok 法國 France

Faatgwok ge 法國嘅 French (in general)

Faatgwok-yàhn 法國人 French (people)

faatleuht 法律 laws, legislation

Faat'mán*/màhn 法文 French (language)

faatyìhng-sī 髮型師 barber

fai 肺 lungs

faiwá* 廢話 nonsense

faiyuhng 費用 cost (expense)

fān (jūng) 分（鐘） minute

fān'gēi 分機 extension (telephone)

fānfaat 分發 hand out

fān-hōi 分開 to divide, split up

fānhòhng* 分行 branch (company)

fānsáu 分手 goodbye, to separate

F

fānláih 婚禮 wedding
fánhùhng-sīk 粉紅色 pink
fanlihn 訓練 training
fan-dāi 瞓低 to lie down
fan-gaau 瞓覺 to sleep
fan-jeuhk 瞓着 asleep
fàhnmouh 墳墓 grave
fātleuhk 忽略 to neglect
fahtfún 罰款 fine (punishment)
Fahtgaau 佛教 Buddhism
Fahtgaau ge 佛教嘅 Buddhist
(in general)
Fahtgaau-tòuh 佛教徒
Buddhist (people)
fáujāk 否則 else: or else
fēi 飛 to fly, ticket
fēigēi 飛機 aeroplane
fēigēi-chèuhng 飛機場 airport
fēi-kéuhngjai-sing ge 非强制嘅
optional
fēifaat 非法 illegal
fēilám* 菲林 film (camera)
Fēileuhtbān 菲律賓
Philippines
Fēileuhtbān-yúh 菲律賓語
Filipino (Tagalog)
fēisèuhng 非常 really (very)
fèih 肥 fat, plump
fèih'neih/leih 肥膩 fatty,
greasy
fèihyūk 肥沃 fertile
fōhohk 科學 science
fójūk 火燭 on fire
fó 火 fire
fóchàaih 火柴 matches
fóchē 火車 train
fóchē-jaahm 火車站 train
station
fósāan 火山 volcano
fo 課 lesson
fochē 貨車 truck
fōngbihn 方便 convenient
fōngfaat 方法 way, method
fōngheung 方向 direction
fōngyìhn 方言 dialect
fóng* 房 room
fōngjouh 仿造 patterned

fōngmahn 訪問 visit
fong 放 to put, to place
fongdaaih 放大 to enlarge
fongsūng 放鬆 to relax
fú 苦 bitter
fúyéuhng 撫養 to raise
children
fu 褲 pants, trousers
fubún 副本 copy
fuyuh 富裕 well off, wealthy
fùhsáu-yī 扶手椅 armchair
fuhmóuh 父母 parents
fuhfún 付款 payment
fuhfún-dāan 付款單 invoice
fuhgahn 附近 around
(nearby)
fuhdāam-dākhéi 負擔得起 to
afford
fuhjaak 負責 to take care of
fuhbaaih 腐敗 corrupt
fuhlaahn 腐爛 rotten
fūichàhn 灰塵 dust
fūisīk 灰色 grey
fūifuhk 恢復 resume
fūkjaahp 複雜 complicated
fūkyan 複印 photocopy, to
photocopy
fuhkchùhng 服從 to obey
fuhkmouh 服務 service
fūnyìhng 歡迎 welcome! to
welcome
fūng 風 wind, breeze
fūnggaak 風格 style
fūnggíng 風景 view,
panorama
fūngmeih-choi 風味菜 cuisine,
style of cooking
fūngsin 風扇 fan (electrical)
fūngkwòhng 瘋狂 crazy
fūngleih 鋒利 sharp
fūngmaht 蜂蜜 honey
fūngsó-jó 封鎖咗 closed
(road)
fùhngyahn 縫紉 to sew
fut 闊 broad, spacious, wide
futdouh 闊度 width
futlohk 闊落 spacious

G

gā 加 to add

gā hēunglíu* ge 加香料嘅 spicy

gāgūng chyúhléih 加工處理 cured, preserved

gāsēuhng 加上 plus

gāyiht 加熱 to heat

gākàhm 家禽 poultry

gātìhng 家庭 family

gāsī 傢私 furniture

gá*dihng 假定 to suppose

gá* ge 假嘅 false (not true)

gá*'mouh ge 假冒嘅 fake (imitation)

gafē 咖啡 coffee

gakèih 假期 holiday (vacation)

gasái 駕駛 to steer

gasái-jāpjiu 駕駛執照 (license for driving)

gachìhn 價錢 cost (price)

gajihk 價值 value (cost)

gāai 街 street

gáai'kyut 解決 to solve a problem

gáaisīk 解釋 to explain

gaaisiuh 介紹 to introduce someone

gaaiyi 介意 to mind, to be displeased

gaaijí 戒指 ring (jewelry)

gaakjái 格仔 square

gāamyuhk 監獄 jail, prison

gáam 減 minus

gáam-bōng* 減磅 to lose weight

gáam-fèih 減肥 to lose weight

gáam-ga 減價 to reduce the price

gáamsíu 減少 to decrease, reduction

gáan 揀 to pick, to choose

gáandāan 簡單 simple (uncomplicated)

gáandyún 簡短 brief

Gáanpòuhjaaih 柬埔寨 Cambodia

Gáanpòuhjaaih ge 柬埔寨嘅 Cambodia (in general)

Gáanpòuhjaaih-yàhn 柬埔寨人 Cambodian (people)

gaantíu* ge 間條嘅 striped

gāaují 膠紙 tape, adhesive

gāautūng 交通 traffic

gāauyihk 交易 to trade, to exchange

gáau-cho 搞錯 mistaken

gáau-wàhn 搞匀 to mix

gáaují 餃子 dumpling

gaau 教 to teach

gaausī 教師 teacher

gaau'tóng*/tòhng 教堂 church

gaauyuhk 教育 education, to educate

gaaují 較剪 scissors

gāi 雞 chicken

gāidáan* 雞蛋 egg

gaijuhk 繼續 to continue

gaisìhng 繼承 to succeed

gaisou 計數 to calculate

gaisou-gēi 計數機 calculator

gaiwaahk 計劃 arrangements, planning, plan

gām 金 gold

gāmsuhk 金屬 metal

gāmmáahn 今晚 tonight

gāmyaht 今日 today

gám*yēung* 咁樣 such

gám-hingcheui 感興趣 interested in

gámchìhng 感情 affection

gám-dou yi'ngoih/oih 感到意外 surprised

gám-dou gīngkèih 感到驚奇 astonished

gám-dou wàihhahm 感到遺憾 to regret

gám-dou hīngfáhn 感到興奮 excited

gámgīk 感激 grateful

gámgok 感覺 feeling

G

gámmouh 感冒 flu
gamjí 禁止 to forbid
gahm-jūng 撳鐘 to ring (bell)
gān 筋 tendon
gān 根 root (of plant)
gāngeui 根據 based on, according to
gān-jyuh 跟住 to follow behind
gán 緊 tight
gán'gāp 緊急 urgent
gánjēung 緊張 tense
gán'gán 僅僅 barely, merely
gahnlòih 近來 presently, nowadays
gāng 羹 soup (spicy stew)
gang-chā 更差 worse
gang-dō 更多 more of (things)
gang-hóu 更好 better
gang-síu ge 更少嘅 less (smaller amount)
gang-waaih 更壞 worse
gāpchán 急診 emergency
gāpdung 急凍 chilled
gáu 九 nine
gáu-sahp 九十 ninety
Gáu-yuht 九月 September
gáu 狗 dog
gaumehng a! 救命啊！ help!
gauh 舊 old (of things)
gauhnín* 舊年 last year
gauhsìh 舊時 in olden times
... ge sìhhauh ... 嘅時候 when, at the time
gēibún 基本 basic
gēichó 基礎 base, foundation
Gēidūk-gaau 基督教 Christianity
Gēidūk-tòuh 基督徒 Christian
gēifōng 飢荒 famine
gēifùh 幾乎 nearly
gēifùh móuh 幾乎冇 barely
gēihei 機器 machine, machinery
gēiwuih 機會 chance, opportunity
gēiyuhk 肌肉 muscle

géi (go) 幾（個）several, how many?
Géi daaih nìhn/lìhn'géi? 幾大年紀 how old?
géidō chín*? 幾多錢 how much?
géidím 幾點 what time
géisìh 幾時 when
géi-sahp 幾十 tens of, multiples of ten
géi/gei'nihm/lihm-bán 紀念品 souvenir
géi/gei'nihm/lihm-bēi 紀念碑 monument
gei 寄 to post, to mail
gei-dāi 記低 to note down
geidāk 記得 to remember
geijé 記者 journalist, reporter
gēng 頸 neck
gēnglín 頸鏈 necklace
geng 鏡 mirror
gēuimàhn 居民 resident, inhabitant
géuibaahn 舉辦 to hold (event)
geui 句 sentence
geuihyìhng 巨型 huge
geuk 腳 foot
geuk'jāahng 腳睜 ankle
geukjí 腳趾 toe
gēung 薑 ginger
gīkhei 激氣 cross, angry
gihk 極 very, extremely
gihksíu 極少 hardly
gímchàh 檢查 to examine, to check, to verify
gīnchìh-dou dái 堅持到底 to stick out
gīnchìh yiukàuh 堅持要求 to press
gīndihng 堅定 firm (definite)
gīn'kyut 堅決 determined, stubborn
ginjūk 建築 architecture
ginlaahp 建立 to establish, to set up
ginmihn 見面 to meet

G

gihn 件 piece, item

gihnhōng 健康 healthy

gihnsān wahnduhng 健身運動 fitness training

gihn 鍵 key (computer)

gihnpùhn 鍵盤 keyboard (of computer)

gīngfai 經費 funds, funding

gīnggwo 經過 pass, go through

gīngjai 經濟 economy

gīngjai sahtwaih 經濟實惠 economical

gīnglēih 經理 manager

gīnglihk 經歷 to experience

gīngsèuhng 經常 always, often, frequent

gīngyihm 經驗 experience

gīngkèih 驚奇 surprised

gīngchaat 警察 police officer

gīngchaat-gūk* 警察局 police

gīnggou 警告 warning, to warn

gingjāng 競爭 to compete

gihp-jyuh 夾住 stuck, won't move

git-jó-fān 結咗婚 married

gitbīng 結冰 freeze

gitchūk 結束 complete (finished)

gitfān 結婚 to marry, to get married

gitgwó 結果 resulting from, as a result

gitsaht 結實 stout

gīu'ngouh/ouh 驕傲 proud

gíujing 矯正 to correct

giujouh 叫做 called, named

giu'haam-sēng 叫喊聲 cry

giu-sēng* 叫醒 to wake someone up

gō(kūk) 歌（曲） song

gōmàih 歌迷 fan (of music)

... gó júng yàhn ... 嗰種人 one who, the one which

gó 嗰 that

gó'bīn/bihn 嗰邊 over there

gódī 嗰啲 those

gódouh 嗰度 there

gósyu 嗰處 there

gòhgō* 哥哥 brother (older)

góibin 改變 to change (conditions, situations)

góibin jyúyi 改變主意 change one's mind

góijing 改正 to correct

goi 蓋 lid

goijēung 蓋章 stamp (ink)

gok-sīk gok-yeuhng 各式各樣 every kind of

gokdāk 覺得 to feel

goklōktáu* 角落頭 corner

goksīk 角色 role

gōn 乾 dry

gōnchou 乾燥 dry (weather)

gōnjehng 乾淨 cleanliness

gōn 肝 liver

gónchēut 趕出 to chase away, to chase out

gōngmùhn 肛門 anus

góng 講 to tell (a story), to say, to speak

góng-daaihwah 講大話 to lie, to tell a falsehood

góng-dāk hóu ngāam/āam 講得好啱 indeed!

góngga 講價 to bargain

góngjoh 講座 lecture

góngsī 講師 lecturer (at university)

góngsiu 講笑 to joke

gong 鋼 steel

got 割 to cut

gōu 高 tall, high

gōudouh 高度 height

gōuhing 高興 glad, happy, pleased

Gōumìhn 高棉 Cambodia

Gōumìhn ge 高棉嘅 Cambodian (in general)

Gōumìhn-yàhn 高棉人 Cambodian (people)

gōuyíhfū-kàuh 高爾夫球 golf

gōu'ngāh/āh 高雅 elegant

gōuyún 睪丸 testicles

gūduhk 孤獨 own, on one's

G

gūhòhn 孤寒 mean (misery), stingy

gūjéung* 姑丈 uncle (husband of father's sister)

gūgū 姑姑 aunt (father's sister, unmarried)

gūmā 姑媽 aunt (father's sister, married)

gúdoih 古代 ancient

gújīk 古蹟 remains (historical)

gúwún* 古玩 antiques

gū 估 to guess

gū*jái 故仔 story (tale)

gu'tái 固體 solid

guhk 焗 to bake

guhklòuh 焗爐 oven

gūngchek 公尺 meter (measure distance)

gūngdouh 公道 reasonable (price)

gūnggūng-pòhpó* 公公婆婆 grandparents (maternal)

gūngguhng 公共 public

gūnggān 公斤 kilogram

gūngléih 公里 kilometer

gūngmàhn 公民 citizen

gūngmouh-yùhn 公務員 officials (government)

gūngpìhng 公平 just, fair, justice

gūngsī 公司 company, firm

gūngsih-bāau 公事包 briefcase

gūng'yuh 公寓 apartment

gūng'yún* 公園 gardens, park

gūngchóng 工廠 factory

gūnggeuih 工具 tool

gūngjeuhng 工匠 craftsperson

gūngjok 工作 job, function, to work

gūngjok-yaht 工作日 working day

gūngyàhn 工人 servant

gūnggīk 攻擊 attack (in war)

gūnghéi (néih/léih) 恭喜(你) congratulations!

Gūnghéi Faatchòih 恭喜發財 Happy (Chinese) New Year!

GW

gwā 瓜 melon

gwáfúh 寡婦 widow

gwa 掛 to hang

gwahouh 掛號 to register

gwahouh-seun 掛號信 registered post

gwa-jyuh 掛住 to miss (loved one)

gwāanfū 鰥夫 widower

gwāanhaih-mòhng 關系網 network

gwāanseui 關税 duty (import tax)

gwāanyū 關於 concerning

gwāigau 歸咎 to blame

gwái 鬼 ghost

gwai 貴 expensive, costly

gwaibān 貴賓 guest of honor

gwaijit 季節 season

gwaihtói* 櫃檯 counter (for paying, buying tickets)

gwaihtúng 櫃桶 drawer

gwāndéui* 軍隊 army, troops

gwan 棍 stick, pole

gwāttàuh 骨頭 bone

gwójāp 果汁 juice

gwójeung 果醬 jam

gwo 過 to cross, to go over

gwosāt 過失 fault

gwo-yé*/yeh 過夜 to stay overnight

gwodāk yuhfaai 過得愉快 enjoy oneself, to

gwofahn jyuyi síujit 過份注意 小節 fussy

gwoheui 過去 past, former

gwokgā 國家 nation, country

gwokjai 國際 international

gwokjai-jeuhngkéi* 國際象棋 chess

gwokjihk 國籍 nationality

Gwokyúh 國語 Mandarin (language)

gwok'ngoih/oih 國外 abroad

gwok'wòhng 國王 king

gwōng 光 light (bright)

gwōngdíp* 光碟 CD

gwōngpún*-yuhtduhk-hei 光盤閱讀器 CD-ROM

gwōngtūk 光禿 bald

gwóngbo 廣播 broadcast, program

gwōngchèuhng 廣場 square, town square

Gwóngdūng ge 廣東嘅 Cantonese (in general)

Gwóngdūng-wá* 廣東話 Cantonese (language)

Gwóngdūng-yàhn 廣東人 Cantonese (people)

Gwóngjāu 廣州 Guangzhou (Canton)

gwuih 瘤 worn out, tired

gwúnléih 管理 manage, succeed

gwun'gwān 冠軍 champion

gwuntáu* 罐頭 can, tin

H

hā 蝦 prawn

hātchī 乞嗤 sneeze

hah yāt go 下一個 next (in line, sequence)

hah (go) sīngkèih 下（個）星期 next week

hah (go) láihbaai 下（個）禮拜 next week

hahmihn 下面 below, under

hah'ngh 下午 afternoon (3 pm to dusk)

hah'ngohk/ohk 下顎 jaw, (lower)

hahpàh 下扒 chin

hàaih 鞋 shoes

háaih 蟹 crab

haak-chān 嚇親 frightened

haakyàhn 客人 guest

haam 喊 to cry, to weep

hàahm 鹹 salty

hàahm-bénggōn 鹹餅乾 biscuit (salty, cracker)

hàahmtàuh 銜頭 title (of person)

hàahng 行 to walk

hàahng-dāk-dou 行得到 walking distance

hàahnglouh heui 行路去 on foot

hāaumùhn 敲門 to knock

háu'hot 口渴 thirsty

háauleuih 考慮 consider (to think over)

háau-sīh 考試 exam, test

haauhgwó 效果 effect, result

hahtīn 夏天 summer

hái 喺 at

hái ngūk/ūk'kéi* 喺 ... 屋企 at home

hái ... yahpbihn 喺 ... 入邊 in, at (space), inside of

hái ... chìhnmihn 喺 ... 前面 in front of

hái ... deuimihn 喺 ... 對面 across from

hái ... hauhmihn 喺 ... 後面 behind

hái ... jīgāan 喺 ... 之間 between

hái ... jījūng 喺 ... 之中 among

hái ... kèihgāan 喺 ... 期間 during

hái ... ngoih/oih'mihn 喺 ... 外面 outside of

hái ... pòhngbīn 喺 ... 旁邊 beside

hái/hēung 喺 / 響 in (time, years)

haih 係 yes

haih mē? 係咩? really?

haihtúng 系統 system

hāk wùhjīu-fán 黑胡椒粉 pepper (black)

hākbohk 刻薄 mean (cruel)

hākfuhk 克服 to overcome

hākséuhng 刻上 to engrave

hāksīk 黑色 black

H

- hàhmwùh 含糊 vague
- hàhmyùhn-dihnyàuh 含鉛電油 leaded petrol
- hángdihng 肯定 sure
- hàhngduhng 行動 action, movement, motion
- hàhnglèih 行李 luggage, baggage
- hahng'wahn 幸運 lucky
- hahp-màaih 合埋 to close, to cover
- hahp-màaih yātchàih 合埋一齊 to join together
- hahpchìhng-hahplèih 合情合理 reasonable (sensible)
- hah-chìhng-lèih 合情理 sensible
- hahpfaat 合法 legal
- hahpgaak 合格 to pass an exam
- hahptùhng 合同 contract
- hahpfùh bīujéun 合符標準 to measure up
- hahpsīk luhkyām-dáai* 盒式錄音帶 cassette
- hàuhlùhng 喉嚨 throat
- háuh 厚 thick (of things)
- hauhfui 後悔 sorry, to feel regretful
- hauhlòih 後來 afterwards, then
- hauhmihn 後面 back, rear
- hauhsāang 後生 young
- hauhsāang-jái'néui*/lèui* 後生仔女 youth (young person)
- hauhyaht 後日 day after tomorrow
- hauhyeuih 後裔 descendant
- hēi 稀 thin (of liquids)
- hēisāng 犧牲 to sacrifice
- hēimohng 希望 to hope, to wish
- hēimohng yáuh hó'nàhng 希望有可能 hopefully
- hēipin 欺騙 to deceive
- héisān 起身 get up (from bed)
- héiyùhn 起源 origin
- hēi(ngūk/ūk) 起（屋）to build

- héi-fáanying 起反應 react to
- héi-jokyuhng 起作用 to work, to function
- héimáh 起碼 at least
- héifūn 喜歡 to be fond of
- hei'hauh 氣候 climate
- heifān 氣氛 atmosphere, ambience
- heiséui 汽水 soft drink
- heifuhk 戲服 costume
- heiyún 戲院 cinema
- hēng 輕 light (not heavy)
- hēuikau 虛構 to make up (a story)
- héui'hó-jing 許可証 permit
- heui 去 to go
- heui bīnsyu 去邊處 where to
- heui bīndouh 去邊度 where to
- hēung 香 fragrant, incense
- Hēunggóng 香港 Hong Kong
- hēungjīu 香蕉 banana
- hēunglíu* 香料 spices
- hēungmàauh 香茅 lemongrass
- hēungséui 香水 perfume
- hēunghá* 鄉下 country (rural area)
- héungsauh 享受 to enjoy
- héung 響 on, at
- héung ... kèihgāan 響 ... 期間 while, during
- héung ... chìhnmihn 響 ... 前面 in front of
- héung ... jīgāan 響 ... 之間 between
- héung ... chìhnmihn 響 ... 前面 before (in front of)
- héung ... ngoih/oih'mihn 響 ... 外面 outside of
- héung ngūk/ūk'kēi* 響 ... 屋企 at home
- héung ... pòhngbīn 響 ... 旁邊 beside
- héung ... hauhmihn 響 ... 後面 behind
- héung ... yahpbihn 響 ... 入邊 inside of
- heung 向 toward (people/place)

H

heung chìhn 向前 forward

heung hah 向下 down, downward

heung-jyuh 向住 head for, toward

heung seuhng 向上 up, upward

him 欠 to owe

hínsih 顯示 to reveal (make known)

hínsih-hei 顯示器 monitor (of computer)

hīngdaih-jímuih 兄弟姐妹 sibling

hingjūk 慶祝 to celebrate

hipdihng 協定 agreement

hipjoh 協助 assistance

hólìhn 可憐 pity

hó'nàhng/làhng 可能 could, may, might, possible, probably

hó'ngoi/oi 可愛 cute, appealing, lovely

hópa 可怕 terrible

hósīk 可惜 what a pity!

hóyíh 可以 be able to

hòh 河 river

hòh'ngohn/ohn 河岸 bank (of river)

hòhlāan-dáu* 荷蘭豆 snowpeas

hōi 開 to turn on, to open

hōichē 開車 leave (train/bus), to drive (a car)

hōi-chēung 開槍 to shoot (with a gun)

hōichí 開始 to start, to begin, beginning

hōisām 開心 happy

hōitàuh 開頭 beginning

hōisyùhn 開船 to sail

hói 海 sea

hóigóng 海港 port, harbor

hói'gwāi 海龜 turtle (sea)

hóihahp 海峽 strait

hóimìhn 海棉 sponge

hóisīn 海鮮 seafood

hóitāan 海灘 beach

hóiwāan 海灣 bay

hóiyàuh 海郵 surface mail

hóiyèuhng 海洋 ocean

hói'ngoih/oih 海外 overseas

hohk 學 to study, to learn

hohkhaauh 學校 school

hohksāang 學生 pupil, student

hōn'gwún 看管 to watch over, to guard

hónyáuh ge 罕有嘅 rare (scarce)

Honjih 漢字 character (Chinese)

Hòhnmàn* 韓文 Korean (language)

Hòhnyúh 韓語 Korean (language)

Hòhn'gwok 韓國 South Korea

Hòhn'gwok-yàhn 韓國人 Korean (South)

hóhnjōi 旱災 drought

hohn 汗 sweat

hōngfuhk 康復 to recover (cured)

hóng* 巷 lane (alley)

hóngkoi 慷慨 generous

hong 烘 toasted

hòhnghàhng 航行 to sail

hòhnghūng-yàauhgín* 航空郵件 airmail

hot 渴 thirsty

hóu 好 well (good), nice

hóu-dī 好啲 better

... hóu-m̀h-hóu a? ... 好唔好呀? let's (suggestion)

hóuchíh 好似 like, as

hóuchói 好彩 fortunately

hóudō 好多 lots of, many, much

hóufaai 好快 soon, quickly

hóugihk laak 好極嘞 wonderful

hóujyún* 好轉 to get better (be cured)

hóusām 好心 kind, good (of persons)

hóusihk 好食 tasty, delicious

hóusíu 好少 seldom

17

H

- hóusiu 好笑 funny
- hóutīn 好天 clear (of weather)
- hòuh 蠔 oyster
- hòuhmáih 毫米 millimeter
- hòuhwàh 豪華 luxurious
- houhmáh 號碼 number
- hūng 胸 chest (breast)
- hūngmáahng 兇猛 fierce
- hūng ge 空嘅 empty
- hūngdeih 空地 field, empty space
- hūnggāan 空間 room, space
- hūnghei 空氣 air
- hūngtiuh 空調 air conditioning
- húnghaak 恐嚇 to threaten
- hungjai 控制 hold back
- hùhng-lòhbaahk 紅蘿蔔 carrot
- hùhngsīk 紅色 red
- hùhngséui 洪水 flood
- hyut 血 blood
- hyut'gwún 血管 blood vessel

J

- jā-dihndāanchē 揸電單車 to ride (motorcycle)
- jadai 咋帝 to pretend
- jaai 債 debt
- jaak 窄 narrow
- jaakgwaai 責怪 to blame
- jaakyahm 責任 responsibility
- jaahm 站 stop (bus, train)
- jaahmsìh 暫時 temporary
- jaan 讚 to praise
- jaahn 賺 to earn
- jāang 爭 to fight over
- jaahpgwaan 習慣 used to
- jaahpjuhk 習俗 custom, tradition
- jaahphahp 集合 to assemble, to gather
- jaahpjūng 集中 to concentrate
- jaahpji 雜誌 magazine
- jaahpsēng 雜聲 noise
- jaauh'yúh 驟雨 shower (of rain)
- jāi 仔 son

- jāi'néui*/léui* 仔女 child (offspring)
- jai 掣 switch
- jaibán 祭品 sacrifice
- jaijouh 製造 to manufacture
- jām 針 needle
- jámtàuh 枕頭 pillow
- jam-tau 浸透 to soak
- jahm-séi 浸死 to drown
- jān 真 true
- jānhaih 真係 really (in fact)
- jānhaih hósīk la! 真係可惜喇 what a shame!
- jānsìhng-gám* 真誠咁 truly
- jānjyū 珍珠 pearl
- jahnyúh 陣雨 shower (of rain)
- jāngleuhn 爭論 argument
- jāng 憎 to hate
- jāng-bóng* 增磅 to gain weight
- jānggā 增加 increase, to increase
- jāngjéung 增長 grow larger, to
- jāp 汁 sauce
- jāp-héi 執起 to pick up something
- jaht 侄 nephew (brother's son)
- jaht'néui*/léui* 侄女 niece (brothers' daughter)
- jahtbehng 疾病 disease
- jāu 洲 continent
- jāumuht 週末 weekend
- jāuwàih 周圍 around (surrounding)
- jáu 走 to run
- jáusī 走私 to smuggle (illegal goods)
- jáu-jó (bāsí, fēigēi) 走咗 (巴士, 飛機) to miss (bus, flight etc.)
- jáulóng* 走廊 corridor
- jáulóu* 走佬 run away
- jáu 酒 alcohol, liquor
- jáubā 酒吧 bar (serving drinks)
- jauhyiu 就要 shall, will
- jē 遮 to cover, umbrella

J

jéfū 姐夫 brother-in-law (wife's older sister's husband)

je 借 to borrow, to lend

je 蔗 sugarcane

jèhjē* 姐姐 sister (older)

jehk 席 mat

jéng 井 well (for water)

jeng 正 beautiful (of things and places)

jēui 追 to chase

jēuikàuh 追求 pursue

jēuikàuh héungsauh 追求享受 to play around

jéui 嘴 mouth

jéuisèuhn 嘴唇 lips

jeui 最 most (superlative)

jeuichā 最差 worst

jeuichìh 最遲 at the latest

jeuichō 最初 original

jeuidō 最多 most (the most of)

jeui'hauh 最後 last (final)

jeuihóu 最好 best

jeuisíu 最少 least (smallest amount)

jeuiwaaih 最壞 worst

jeuihfáan* 罪犯 criminal

jéuk* 雀 bird

jeuk 著 to wear (clothes)

jeukchàauh 雀巢 nest

jeuhkluhk 着陸 land, to (plane)

jēun 樽 bottle

jéunbeih 準備 to prepare, to make ready

jéunbeih-hóu 準備好 prepared, ready

jéunhéui 準許 to permit, to allow

jéunsìh 準時 punctual

jeunháu-fo 進口貨 import

jeunbouh-jó 進步咗 to get better (improve)

jeun-yāt-bouh 進一步 further, additional

jeuhn só'nàhng/làhng 盡所能 do one's best

jeuhnlihk 盡力 to make an effort

jēung 將 will, shall

jēunglòih 將來 in future

jéungdaaih 長大 grow up (child)

jéungbui 長輩 elder

jeuhngfū 丈夫 husband

jeuhngkéi* 象棋 Chinese chess

jeuhng'ngàh/àh 象牙 ivory

jeuhnggāau 橡膠 rubber (material)

jīchìh 支持 to back up

jīchìhn 之前 beforehand, earlier

jīhauh 之後 after

jīdou 知道 know, be informed

jīgaak 資格 qualification

jī'màh 芝麻 sesame seeds

jīsí 芝士 cheese

jīsai 姿勢 gesture

jīgūng 子宮 uterus

jíchēut 指出 point out

jífāi 指揮 to command

jígaap 指甲 nail (finger, toe)

jíjaak 指責 to accuse

jísih 指示 instruct, tell to do something

jí(haih) 只（係）just, only

jí 紙 paper

jí'háp* 紙盒 box (cardboard)

jísīk 紫色 purple

jítùhng 紫銅 copper

jisīk 知識 knowledge

jisíu 至少 at least

jihdín 字典 dictionary

jihmóuh 字母 alphabet

jihtìuh 字條 note (written)

jihchùhng 自從 since

jihgéi 自己 self

jihgéi ge 自己嘅 own, personal

jihhòuh 自豪 pride

jihjyūn-sām 自尊心 self-respect/self-esteem

jih'ngóh/óh gaaisiuh 自我介紹 to introduce oneself

jihyàuh 自由 free, freedom

jihyìhn fūnggíng 自然風景 scenery

J

jihyìhn ge 自然嘅 natural

jih'lìuh 治療 cure (medical)

jih'yún 寺院 temple (Chinese)

jīkhāk 即刻 at once

jīkyihp 職業 profession, occupation

jihk 直 straight (not crooked)

jihkdou 直到 until

jihkdāk 值得 to be worth

jihkmaht 植物 plant

jihkmaht-yùhn 植物園 botanic gardens

jīmdyūn 尖端 tip (end) point, dot

jimyáuh 佔有 to possess

jīn 氈 blanket

jīn 煎 to fry

jinjāng 戰爭 war

jīng ge 蒸嘅 steamed

jīnghei 蒸汽 steam

jīnglihk 精力 energy

jíng go 整個 whole, to be complete

jíng-gōnjehng 整乾淨 to clean

jíng-chē-chóng 整車廠 garage (for repairs)

jíngchàih 整齊 neat, orderly

jínggit 整潔 tidy

jingfōng-yìhng 正方形 square (shape)

jingkok 正確 right, correct

jingsèuhng 正常 normal

jingsīk 正式 official, formal

jingdóng 政黨 party (political)

jingfú 政府 government

jingjih 政治 politics

jinggeui 証據 proof

jingmìhng 証明 to prove

jingsyū 証書 certificate

jingyàhn 証人 witness

jihng 靜 silent

jihnghaih 淨係 only

jihng-lohk ge 剩落嘅 rest, remainder

jip 接 to pick up someone

jip-dihnwá* 接電話 answer the phone

jipgahn 接近 to approach (in space)

jipsauh 接受 to accept

jitmuhk 節目 program, schedule

jityaht 節日 festival

jīujóu 朝早 early in the morning

jīupàaih 招牌 signboard

jīusáu 招手 to wave

jiugu 照顧 to take care of

jiuh 嚼 to chew

jiuhgin 召見 call, summon

jó'bīn/bihn 左邊 left-hand side

... jóyáu* ... 左右 around (approximately)

jójí 阻止 to prevent, bar (blocking way)

jó'ngoih/oih 阻礙 hindrance, to hinder

johwái* 座位 seat

jōi'naahn/laahn 災難 disaster

joi 再 again

joi làih yāt go 再嚟一個 another (same again)

joigin 再見 goodbye

jokgā 作家 writer

jokmán* 作文 composition, writings

jōng-fo 裝貨 to load up

jōng-múhn 裝滿 to fill

jōngsīk 裝飾 to decorate

jōngsīk-bán 裝飾品 ornament

jong 壯 strong

jongláih 葬禮 funeral

johng 撞 collision, to collide

johng-chē 撞車 crashed (car)

johngfong 狀況 condition (status)

jōu 租 to rent, to hire

jóu 早 early

jóuchāan 早餐 breakfast, morning meal

jóusīn 祖先 ancestor

jouh 做 to do, to act, to make, to work

jouh-màaih 做埋 to finish off

jouh-yùhn 做完 to finish, to complete

K

jouh-dāk hóu! 做得好 well done!

jūk néih/leih hóuwahn 祝你好運 best wishes! good luck!

jūk-jyuh 捉住 to hold (grasp), to catch

jūk-dóu* 捉到 to capture

jūkgau 足夠 enough

jūkkàuh 足球 soccer

juhkjihm 逐漸 gradually

jūnghohksāang 中學生 secondary school student

jūnggāan 中間 center, middle

Jūnggwok 中國 China

Jūnggwok ge 中國嘅 Chinese (in general)

Jūnggwok-yàhn 中國人 Chinese (people)

jūnghohksāang 中學生 secondary school student

jūngjyún-jaahm 中轉站 connection (transport)

Jūngmán*/Jūngmàhn 中文 Chinese (language)

Jūngmàhn-jih 中文字 Chinese characters

jūng'ngh 中午 afternoon (midday)

jūngyēung 中央 central

jūnggaau 宗教 religion

jūng 鐘 clock

jūngtàuh 鐘頭 hour

jūngyi 鐘意 to be fond of, to prefer

jūngjí 終止 end (finish)

jūngyū 終於 finally

júngleuih 種類 type, sort, class, category

júngjí 種子 seed

júngléih 總理 prime minister

júngtúng 總統 president

jung 種 to grow, to cultivate

jung'waaih-jó 縱壞咗 spoiled (of children)

juhng meih 仲未 not yet

juhngsih 重視 to value

julɯgyiu 重要 important

juhngyiu-sing 重要性 importance

jyūgūlīk 朱古力 chocolate

jyūgūlīk-sīk 朱古力色 brown (coffee color)

jyū 豬 pig

jyūyuhk 豬肉 pork

jyúgēi 主機 computer (main)

jyúyi 主意 idea

jyúyiu 主要 main, most important

jyúyiu ge 主要嘅 mainly

jyúyàhn 主人 host

jyú 煮 to boil

jyú-gwo ge 煮過嘅 boiled

jyú-faahn 煮飯 to cook (rice)

jyú-suhk-jó 煮熟咗 cooked

jyú-sung 煮餸 to cook (dishes)

jyú-tau 煮透 well-cooked, well-done

jyu-yahp 注入 to pour, to inject

jyuyi 注意 to notice

jyuh 住 live (stay in a place)

jyuhsūk 住宿 accommodation

jyūn'gā 專家 expert

jyūn'ging 尊敬 to respect

jyūnjuhng 尊重 respect

jyún 轉 to switch, to change

jyun-chē 轉車 to change (bus/train)

jyunsehk 鑽石 diamond

K

kaaugahn 靠近 close to, nearby

kaau-gán 靠緊 close together, tight

kaiyeuk 契約 contract

kàhm/chàhm'yaht 琴/尋日 yesterday

kàhmmáahn 琴晚 last night

kàhnlihk 勤力 hardworking, industrious

kàhn 近 close to, nearby

kāp 吸 to suck

kāpyáhn 吸引 attract

K

kāt 咳 to cough

kātsēng 咳聲 cough

kāt-yeuhksēui 咳藥水 cough syrup

káhmmóuh 舅母 aunt (wife of mother's older/younger brother)

káuhfú* 舅父 uncle (mother's brother)

káuhjái 舅仔 brother-in-law (wife's younger brother)

kèh-máh 騎馬 to ride (horse)

kèih 旗 flag

kèihdahk 奇特 fancy

kèih'gwaai 奇怪 strange

kèihsaht 其實 actually

kèihtā 其他 other

kèihtóu 祈禱 prayer, to pray

kèihmohng 期望 to expect

kéih 企 to stand

kéih-hēisān 企起身 to stand up

kéihtòuh 企圖 attempt

kéuih 佢 he, him, she, her

kéuihdeih 佢哋 they, them

kéuihdeih ge 佢哋嘅 their, theirs

kéuih ge 佢嘅 her, hers

kéuihjyuht 拒絕 refusal, to refuse

kéuihlèih 距離 distance

keuhk'yún 劇院 theater (drama)

kèuhngbīk 強迫 force, compel

kèuhngdaaih 強大 powerful

kéuhngjai-sing ge 強制性嘅 compulsory

kīng-gái 傾偈 to talk

kìuh 橋 bridge

kokdihng 確定 sure

koksaht 確實 exact, exactly

kokyihng 確認 confirm

kongyíh 抗議 to protest

kūkkèih 曲奇 cookie, sweet biscuit

kùhng 窮 poor (not rich)

kyùhnleih 權利 rights

kyùhnlihk 權力 authority (power)

kyùhnwāi 權威 authority (person)

kyutdihng 決定 decision, to decide

kyutdím 缺點 defect

kyutfaht 缺乏 scarce

kyutjihk 缺席 absent

kyutsíu 缺少 lacking

KW

kwāijāk 規則 rules

kwāi'kwāi-géuigéui 規規矩矩 well-behaved

kwan'nàahn/làahn 困難 difficult

kwāhn 裙 skirt

kwongchyùhn-sēui 礦泉水 mineral water

L

lāai 拉 to pull

láai 舔 to lick

láam 籃 basket

láam-jyuh 攬住 to embrace

làahm'bīn/bihn 南邊 south

Làahm'hòhn 南韓 South Korea

làahm-pàhngyáuh 男朋友 boyfriend

làahmjái 男仔 boy

làahmsing 男性 male

làahmyàn* 男人 man

làahn'gwo 難過 sad

làahndāk 難得 rarely, seldom

làahnwàihchìhng 難為情 embarrassed

làahmkàuh 籃球 basketball

làahmsīk 籃色 blue

láahndoh 懶惰 lazy

lāang 冷 wool (for knitting)

láahng 冷 cold

laahphāk 立刻 right now, immediately

laahpsaap 垃圾 garbage

laahp 臘 wax

laahpjūk 臘燭 candle

laahtjīu 辣椒 pepper (chilli)

laahtjīu-jeung 辣椒醬 chilli sauce

làih 泥 mud

làih'tóu 泥土 earth, soil

làih 嚟 to come

làih-gán 嚟緊 on the way

làihmìhng 黎明 dawn

làih-yuhtgīng 嚟月經 to menstruate

láihbaai 禮拜 week

Láihbaai-luhk 禮拜六 Saturday

Láihbaai-ńgh 禮拜五 Friday

Láihbaai-sāam 禮拜三 Wednesday

Láihbaai-sei 禮拜四 Thursday

Láihbaai-yaht 禮拜日 Sunday

Láihbaai-yih 禮拜二 Tuesday

Láihbaai-yāt 禮拜一 Monday

láihmaauh 禮貌 courtesy, manners

láihmaht 禮物 gift

láihtòhng 禮堂 hall

laihjī 荔枝 lychee

laihjí 例子 example

laihyùh 例如 such as, for example

làhnglihk 能力 ability

lāu 嬲 angry

láu* 樓 floor

làuhhah 樓下 downstairs

làuhseuhng 樓上 upstairs

làuhtāi 樓梯 stairs

làuhtāi-kāp 樓梯級 steps, stairs

làuhtēng 樓廳 circle (theater seats)

làuh-chyùhn 留存 leave behind for safekeeping

làuh-dāi 留低 leave behind on purpose

làuhsūk 留宿 to stay overnight

làuhyi 留意 to pay attention

làuhyìhn 留言 message

làuhyìhn-gēi 留言機 answering machine

làuhhàhng 流行 popular

làuh'hyut 流血 to bleed

làuhleih 流利 fluent

lauh-jó 漏咗 leave behind by accident

lauhsēui 漏水 to leak

lēi-màaih 呢埋 to hide

lēi 梨 pear

lèih'lùhng 尼龍 nylon

lèih-fān 離婚 to divorce

lèihhōi 離開 to depart

lèih-jó-fān 離咗婚 divorced

lèihbā 籬笆 fence

léih 你 you

léih'deih 你哋 you (plural)

léih hóu 你好！ hello, hi

léih hóu ma 你好嗎 how are you?

leihsīk 利息 interest (bank)

leihyeuhn 利潤 profit

leih 脷 tongue

leng 靚 beautiful (of things and places)

lengjái 靚仔 beautiful (of man)

leng'néui*/léui* 靚女 beautiful (of woman)

lёhngtāai 領呔 tie, necktie

lёui* 女 daughter

lёuih'jái 女仔 girl

lёuih'jōng-sēutsāam 女裝恤衫 blouse

lёuih-pàhngyáuh 女朋友 girlfriend

lёuih'sai 女婿 son-in-law

lёuih'sàhn 女神 goddess

lёuih'sih 女仕 lady

lёuihsing ge 女性嘅 female

lёuih'wòhng 女王 queen

lёuih'yán* 女人 woman

lёuihchìhng 旅程 trip, journey

lёuihgwún 旅館 hotel

lёuihhaak 旅客 traveler, tourist

L

léuihhàhng 旅行 trip, journey

léuihyàuh-jí'nàahm/làahm 旅遊指南 guidebook

léuihmihn 裡面 inside

lèuhn'gēui 鄰居 neighbor

lèuhng'hàaih 涼鞋 sandals

lèuhngsōng 涼爽 cool

lèuhng-yāt-lèuhng 涼一涼 to cool

lèuhng 量 to measure

léuhng 兩 two (measure)

léuhng chi 兩次 twice

léuhng (go) 兩（個） both

léuhng go dōu m̀h'haih 兩個都唔係 neither

leuhtsī 律師 lawyer

lī 呢 this

līdī 呢啲 these

lī'douh 呢度 here

lī'syu 呢處 here

lihk 力 strength, force

lihksí 歷史 history

lìhn 年 year

lìhn'géi 年紀 age

lìhn'géi daaih-dī ge 年紀大啲嘅 elder

lìhn'hēng 年輕 young

lìhn'hēng-yàhn 年輕人 young (young person)

lìhn'lìhng 年齡 age

lìhn 連 even (also)

lìhnjip 連接 to connect together

lìhnjip-dím 連接點 connection (transport)

lìhn'nǎai/lǎai 煉奶 condensed milk

lihnjaahp 練習 practice, to practice

lìhng'hó 寧可 rather than

lìhngjihng 寧靜 peaceful

lìhng 零 zero

lìhnggín* 零件 part (of machine)

lìhng'mūng 檸檬 lemon, citrus

líhngdouh 領導 lead (to be a leader)

líhngdouh-yàhn 領導人 leader

líhngsih-gwún 領事館 consulate

lihng yàhn hīngfáhn 令人興奮 exciting

lihng yàhn jok'ngáu/áu 令人作嘔 disgusting

lihng yàhn yuhfaai 令人愉快 pleasant

lihng yàhn wàih'nàahn/làahn 令人為難 embarrassing

lihng yàhn gám-dou yi'ngoih/óih 令人感到意外 surprising

lihng'ngoih/oih 另外 other (alternative)

lithōi 裂開 cracked

lihtjáu 烈酒 spirits, hard liquor

Lìuhgwok 寮國 Laos

Lìuhgwok-yàhn 寮國人 Laotian

líuhgáai 瞭解 to realize, to be aware of

liuh 尿 urine

lōyáu 囉柚 bottom (buttocks)

ló 攞 to bring, to carry, to fetch

ló-jáu 攞走 to remove

lótái 裸體 naked, nude

lòhsī-pāi 螺絲批 screw-driver

lòhsyùhn-yìhng 螺旋形 spiral

loh'máih 糯米 glutinous rice

lòihlàhm 來臨 to approach (in time)

lòihwùih-piu 來回票 return ticket

lòihyùhn 來源 source

lòihyùhn yū 來源於 to originate, to come from

loih 耐 long (time)

loih'sām 耐心 patient (calm)

loih'chyùhn 內存 RAM (computer)

loih'gau 內疚 to feel guilty

lohk-chē 落車 to get off (bus/train)

lohk-syùhn 落船 to get off (boat)

M

lohkhauh 落後 backward
lohk-syut 落雪 to snow
lohk-yúh 落雨 to rain
lohng-gōn 晾乾 dry out (in the sun)
lòuhtàuh 爐頭 stove, cooker
lóuh 老 old (of persons)
lóuhbáan 老闆 boss, shopkeeper
lóuhchāu 老抽 soy sauce (sweet)
lóuhfú 老虎 tiger
lóuhpòh 老婆 wife
lóuhsyú 老鼠 rat
lóuh 腦 mind, brain
lóuh'lihk 努力 effort
louh 路 road
louhchìhng 路程 journey
louhgīng 路經 via
louhpáai* 路牌 sign, road
luhk 六 six
luhk-sahp 六十 sixty
Luhk-yuht 六月 June
luhksīk 綠色 green
luhkyām 錄音 tape recording
luhkyíng-gēi 錄音機 VCR
luhkyàuh 陸郵 surface mail
lūng 窿 hole
lùhng 濃 thick (of liquids)
lùhng 聾 deaf
lyùhnfūn-wúi* 聯歡會 party (event)
lyùhnlok 聯絡 contact, connection
lyúhn 暖 warm, warmth
lyuhn 亂 confusing
lyuhn-chāt-baat-jōu 亂七八糟 in a mess

M

màhfàahn 麻煩 trouble, troublesome
màhjeuk 麻雀 mahjong
màh'má*-déi* 麻麻地 average (so-so, just okay)
màh'muhk 麻木 numb

màhyàuh 麻油 sesame oil
màhmā 媽媽 mother
máh 馬 horse
máhchē 馬車 cart (horsecart)
máhseuhng 馬上 at once, right now
máhlāu 馬騮 monkey
Máhlòihsāi'nga/a 馬來西亞 Malaysia
Máhlòihsāi'nga/a-yàhn 馬來西亞人 Malaysian (people)
Máhlòihsāi'nga/a ge 馬來西亞嘅 Malaysian (in general)
máaih 買 to buy
máaih-dākdóu* 買得到 available (for purchased)
máaih-yéh 買嘢 to shop, go shopping
maaih 賣 to sell
maaih-jó 賣咗 sold
maaih-yùhn 賣完 sold out
màaih-dāan 埋單 to pay bill
máahndím 晚點 delayed (train, bus etc)
máahnfaahn 晚飯 dinner, evening meal
maahn 萬 ten thousand
maahn 慢 slow
maahnmáan*-déi* 慢慢地 slowly
maat-gōn 抹乾 to wipe clean
māau 貓 cat
màauhlìuh 茅寮 shack
maauhyihk 貿易 trade
màihlouh 迷路 lost (can't find way)
màih'nēih/lēih 迷你 mini
máih 米 rice (uncooked grains)
mahksēui 墨水 ink
mahksēui-bāt 墨水筆 pen
mān 蚊 mosquito
màhn 聞 to smell
màhn'geuih 文具 stationery
màhn'gín* 文件 document, letter
màhnfa 文化 culture
mahnhohk 文學 literature

M

màhnjēung 文章 article (in newspaper/journal)

màhnjuhk fuhkjōng 民族服裝 costume

màhn 吻 kiss

mahn 問 to enquire

mahnhauh 問候 say hello

mahntàih 問題 question, problem

màtyéh 乜嘢 what

maht 襪 socks

máuhchyu 某處 somewhere

mē wá* 咩話 pardon me? what did you say?

Mèihgwok 美國 United States

Mèihgwok ge 美國嘅 American (in general)

Mèihgwok-yàhn 美國人 American (people)

méih 尾 tail

meih 未 not yet

meihfān-chāi 未婚妻 fiance

meihfān-fū 未婚夫 fiance

meihsuhk 未熟 unripe

meihdouh 味道 flavor, taste

meihjīng 味精 MSG

mèng* 名 given name

m̀h 唔 not

m̀h'gányiu 唔緊要 never mind!

m̀h'gin-jó 唔見咗 to lose, to mislay

m̀h'gōi 唔該 thank you (service)

m̀h'gōi jeje 唔該借借 excuse me! (getting past)

m̀h'haih 唔係 no, not (with verbs and adjectives)

m̀h'haih ... yauh m̀h'haih ... 唔係 ... 又唔係 ... neither ... nor ...

m̀h'hōisām 唔開心 upset, unhappy

m̀h'hóu 唔好 don't!

m̀h'hóu haakhei 唔好客氣 don't mention it!

m̀h'hóu joi gám*yéung* 唔好再咁樣 stop it!

m̀h'hóuchói 唔好彩 unfortunately, misfortune

m̀h'hóuwahn 唔好運 bad luck

m̀h'léih 唔理 to ignore

m̀h'ngāam/āam 唔啱 wrong (false)

m̀h'sái haakhei 唔駛客氣 you're welcome!

m̀h'syūfuhk 唔舒服 ill, sick

m̀h'tùhng 唔同 different, other

mìhnbou 棉布 cotton

mìhnfā 棉花 cotton wool

mìhnfai 免費 free of charge

Míhndihn 緬甸 Burma

Míhndihn ge 緬甸嘅 Burmese (in general)

Míhndihn-yàhn 緬甸人 Burmese (people)

mihn 臉 face

mihn 麵 noodles

mihnbāau 麵包 bread

mihnfán 麵粉 flour

mihndeui 面對 to face

mihn'geuih 面具 mask

mihnjí 面子 face (respect)

mihnjyūdān 面珠墩 cheek

mìhngdāan 名單 list

mìhngpàaih 名牌 brand name

mìhng 明 understand

mìhnghín 明顯 apparent

mìhngji 明智 sensible

mìhngkok 明確 definite

mìhng'nín*/lín* 明年 next year

mìhngseun-pín* 明信片 postcard

mihnglihng 命令 order (command), to order

mìuhsē 描寫 to describe

míuhtíuh 苗條 slim

míuh 秒 second (instant)

mōdá 摩打 motor, engine

mó 摸 to touch

mòhgū 蘑菇 mushrooms

mōkpèih 剝皮 to peel

mōnggwó 芒果 mango

mòhng 忙 busy (doing something)

mòhnggei 忘記 to forget

mōhng 網 net

mōhngjaahm 網站 website

mōhngkàuh 網球 tennis

móu 帽 hat

mòuhfóng 模仿 to copy

mòuhgān 毛巾 towel

mòuh-haahnjai 無限制 free of restraints

mòuhjī 無知 ignorant

mòuhleuhn hòh sìh ... 無論何時 whenever

mòuhlìuh 無聊 bored

mòuhyùhn-dihnyàuh 無鉛電油 unleaded petrol

móuh 冇 without, no, not (with nouns)

móuhcho 冇錯 exactly! just so!

móuh hó'nàhng/làhng 冇可能 impossible

móuh láihmaauh 冇禮貌 rude, impolite

móuhyàhn 冇人 nobody

móuhyéh 冇嘢 nothing

móuh yisī 冇意思 boring

móuhyuhng 冇用 impossible

móuhhei 武器 weapon

móuhwúi* 舞會 dance

móuhyuhk 侮辱 insult, to insult someone

mouhpàaih-fo 冒牌貨 false (imitation)

mouh 霧 fog

mùihmúi* 妹妹 sister (younger)

múih 每 each, every

múih chi 每次 every time

múih go yàhn 每個人 everybody, everyone

múih go láihbaai 每個禮拜 weekly

múih go sīngkèih 每個星期 weekly

múihdōng ... 每當 ... whenever

múihjāu 每週 weekly

múihmáahn 每晚 nightly

múih'nìhn/lìhn yāt chi 每年一次 annual

muihfū 妹夫 brother-in-law (wife's younger sister's husband)

muhkchìhn 目前 at the present moment

muhkdīk 目的 goal, purpose

muhkdīk-deih 目的地 destination

muhkjai ge 木製嘅 wooden

muhktàuh 木頭 wood

muhk'ngūk/ūk 木屋 hut, shack

muhksī 牧師 priest (Anglican)

mùhn 門 door

múhn 滿 full

múhnyi ge 滿意 satisfied

múhnjūk 滿足 satisfied, to satisfy

muhn 悶 dull (boring)

muhng 夢 dream

N

nàahm'bīn/bihn 南邊 south

Nàahmhòhn 南韓 South Korea

nàahm-pàhngyáuh 男朋友 boyfriend

nàahmjái 男仔 boy

nàahmsing 男性 male

nàahmyán* 男人 man

nàahn'gwo 難過 sad

nàahndāk 難得 rarely, seldom

nàahnwàihchìhng 難為情 embarrassed

nàih 泥 mud

nàihtóu 泥土 earth, soil

nàhnglihk 能力 ability

nāu 嬲 angry

nēi-màaih 呢埋 to hide

nèihlùhng 尼龍 nylon

néih 你 you

néihdeih 你哋 you (plural)

néih hóu 你好！ hello, hi

néih hóu ma 你好嗎 how are you?

néui* 女 daughter

néuihjái 女仔 girl

néuihjōng-sēutsāam 女裝恤衫 blouse

néuih-pàhngyáuh 女朋友 girlfriend

néuihsai 女婿 son-in-law

néuihsàhn 女神 goddess

néuihsih 女士 lady

néuihsing ge 女性嘅 female

néuihwòhng 女王 queen

néuihyán* 女人 woman

nī 呢 this

nīdī 呢啲 these

nīdouh 呢度 here

nīsyu 呢處 here

nìhn 年 year

nìhngéi 年紀 age

nìhngéi daaih-dī ge 年紀大啲嘅 elder

nìhnhēng 年輕 young

nìhnhēng-yàhn 年輕人 young (young person)

nìhnlìhng 年齡 age

nìhnghó 寧可 rather than

nìhngjing 寧靜 peace, peaceful

nìhngmūng 檸檬 lemon, citrus

niuh 尿 urine

nohmáih 糯米 glutinous rice

noih 耐 long (time)

noihsām 耐心 patient (calm)

noihchyùhn 內存 RAM (computer)

noihgau 內疚 to feel guilty

nóuh 腦 mind, brain

nóuhlihk 努力 effort

nùhng 濃 thick (of liquids)

nyūhn 暖 warm, warmth

NG

ńgh 五 five

ńgh-sahp 五十 fifty

Ńgh-yuht 五月 May

ńghchāan 午餐 lunch, midday meal

Ngajāu 亞洲 Asia

ngàh 牙 tooth, teeth

ngàhcháat* 牙刷 toothbrush

ngàhgōu 牙膏 toothpaste

ngaahk'ngoih/oih ge 額外嘅 extra

ngāamsān 啱身 suitable, fitting

ngàhmduhng 岩洞 cave

ngàahnsīk 顏色 colour

ngáahn 眼 eye

ngáahnfahn 眼瞓 sleepy

ngáahngéng* 眼鏡 eyeglasses, spectacles

ngáahnleuih 眼淚 tears

ngáahnmèih 眼眉 eyebrow

ngáahnmèih-mòuh 眼眉毛 eyelashes

ngaahng 硬 hard, stiff

ngaahngpùhn 硬盤 hard disk/drive (computer)

ngaahngjí-bán 硬紙板 cardboard

ngaai(gāau) 嗌（交）to argue

ngaaklihk 壓力 pressure

ngaahktàuh 額頭 forehead

ngāam 啱 correct

ngāamsān 啱身 fitting, suitable

ngāam'ngāam 啱啱 just now

ngaan 晏 late at night

ngaanjau 晏晝 midday

ngaap 鴨 duck

ngáau'tyúhn 拗斷 to break apart

ngáauh 咬 to bite

ngái 矮 short (not tall)

ngái'gwā 矮瓜 eggplant, aubergine

ngàihhím 危險 danger, dangerous

ngaihseuht 藝術 art

ngaihseuht-gā 藝術家 artist

ngāk(yàhn) 呃（人）to cheat

ngam 暗 dark

ngàhn 銀 silver

ngàhnbāau 銀包 wallet, purse

ngàhnjí 銀紙 note (currency)

ngàhnhòhng 銀行 bank (finance)

ngáu 嘔 to vomit

Ngāujāu 歐洲 Europe

O

ngáuhyĭhn 偶然 by chance

ngáuhyĭhn-gāan 偶然間 occasionally

ngàuh'náaih/láaih 牛奶 milk

ngàuhyuhk 牛肉 beef

ngàuh'ná/lá 牛乸 cow

ngàuhyàuh 牛油 butter

ngh'wuih 誤會 misunderstanding

ngố* 鵝 goose

ngòh 蛾 moth

ngóh 我 I, me

ngóhdeih 我哋 we, us

ngóhdeih ge 我哋嘅 our

ngóh ge 我嘅 my, mine

ngoh 餓 hungry

ngohkhei 樂器 musical instrument

ngoi 愛 to love

ngoi'hou 愛好 hobby

ngoichĭhng 愛情 love

ngoiwuh 愛護 to care for, to love

Ngoiyĭhlàahn 愛爾蘭 Ireland

Ngoiyĭhlàahn- yàhn 愛爾蘭人 Irish

Ngoiyĭhlàahn ge 愛爾蘭嘅 Irish (in general)

ngoihgūng 外公 grandfather (maternal)

ngoihfú* 外父 father-in-law

ngoihgwok ge 外國嘅 foreign

ngoihgwok-yàhn 外國人 foreigner

ngoihmaauh 外貌 appearance, looks

ngoihmihn 外面 outside

ngoihmóu* 外母 mother-in-law

ngoihpòh 外婆 grandmother (maternal)

ngoihsāng 外甥 nephew (son of father's sisters/mother's siblings)

ngoihsāng'néui*/léui* 外甥女 niece (daughter of father's sisters)

ngoihtou 外套 jacket

ngoihyī 外衣 coat, jacket

ngohkfú* 岳父 father-in-law

ngohkmóu* 岳母 mother-in-law

ngonmō 按摩 to massage

ngōnchyùhn 安全 secure, safe

ngōnjihng 安靜 quiet

ngōnpàaih 安排 to organize, to arrange

Ngoujāu 澳洲 Australia

Ngoujāu- yàhn 澳洲人 Australian (people)

Ngojāu ge 澳洲嘅 Australian (in general)

Ngoumún* 澳門 Macau

ngūk 屋 house

ngūkdéng* 屋頂 roof

ngūkkéi* 屋企 home, house

O

ố* 鵝 goose

òh 蛾 moth

óh 我 I, me

óhdeih 我哋 we, us

óhdeih ge 我哋嘅 our

óh ge 我嘅 my, mine

oh 餓 hungry

oi 愛 to love

oi'hou 愛好 hobby

oi'chĭhng 愛情 love

oi'wuh 愛護 to care for, to love

Oi'yĭhlàahn 愛爾蘭 Ireland

Oi'yĭhlàahn- yàhn 愛爾蘭人 Irish

Oi'yĭhlàahn ge 愛爾蘭嘅 Irish (in general)

oih'gūng 外公 grandfather (maternal)

oih'fú* 外父 father-in-law

oih'gwok ge 外國嘅 foreign

oih'gwok-yàhn 外國人 foreigner

oih'maauh 外貌 appearance, looks

oih'mihn 外面 outside

oih'móu* 外母 mother-in-law

O

oih'pòh 外婆 grandmother (maternal)

oih'sāng 外甥 nephew (son of father's sisters/mother'siblings)

oih'sāng'néui*/lēui* 外甥女 niece (daughter of father's sisters)

oih'tou 外套 jacket

oih'yī 外衣 coat, jacket

ohk'fū* 岳父 father-in-law

ohk'mōu* 岳母 mother-in-law

ohkkei 樂器 musical instrument

ōn'chyùhn 安全 secure, safe

ōn'jihng 安靜 quiet

ōn'pàaih 安排 to organize, to arrange

on'gām 按金 advance money, deposit

on'mō 按摩 to massage

Ou'jāu 澳洲 Australia

Ou'jāu- yàhn 澳洲人 Australian (people)

Ou'jāu ge 澳洲嘅 Australian (in general)

Ou'mún* 澳門 Macau

Ou'wahn-wúi* 奧運會 Olympics

P

pa 怕 be scared, afraid

pàh 扒 to pickpocket

pàhsáu 扒手 pickpocket

pàh-séuhng 爬上 climb onto

pàaih 排 row

pàaih-dēui* 排隊 queue, to line up

pàaihmìhng 排名 ranking

pàaihjiu 牌照 license, permit

paak-chē 泊車 to park a car

paakdong 拍檔 partner (in business)

paakmaaih 拍賣 to auction

pāandāng 攀登 climb up (hills, mountains)

paangtiuh 烹調 cooking, cuisine

pàahngjeung 膨漲 expand, grow larger

pāauhei 拋棄 to desert, to abandon

panmouh-hei 噴霧器 spray

pàhnjehk ge 貧瘠嘅 barren

pàhngyáuh 朋友 friend

pēpáai* PAIR 牌 cards, game

pèhng 平 cheap, inexpensive

peigú 屁股 buttocks

peiyùh 譬如 example, for

pēi* 皮 leather

pèihdáai* 皮帶 belt

pèihfū 皮膚 skin

pèihgīp 皮夾 suitcase

péihpōu 被舖 bedding

pīnjīk 編織 to weave

pīnjouh 編造 to make up, to invent

pinjí 騙子 cheat, someone who cheats

pingyām 拼音 combine sounds into syllables

pìhng 平 flat, smooth

pìhngdeih 平地 plain (level ground)

pìhngdáng 平等 equal, equality

pìhnggwān 平均 average (numbers)

pìhngjihng 平靜 still, calm, quiet

pìhngsèuhng 平常 usual

pìhngyùhn 平原 plain (level ground)

pìhng'waaht 平滑 smooth (of surfaces)

pìhnggīk 評擊 attack (with words)

pìhnggwó 蘋果 apple

pìhngmohk 屏幕 screen (of computer)

po'waaih 破壞 to destroy

pòhpō* 婆婆 grandmother (maternal)

poksou 樸素 modest, simple

pòhngbīn 旁邊 next to

póupin 普遍 general, all-purpose

pŏupin-gám* 普遍咁 generally

pŏutūng 普通 common, frequent

Pŏutūng-wá* 普通話 Mandarin (language)

poutáu* 舖頭 store, shop

pòuhtòuh-jáu 葡萄酒 wine

(pòuh) tàihjí （葡）提子 grapes

pŏu'yun 抱怨 to complain

pui'hahp 配合 to fit

pui'ngáuh/áuh 配偶 spouse

pùih 陪 to accompany

S

sā 沙 sand

sā'mohk 沙漠 desert (arid land)

sāyùh 鯊魚 shark

sāaichín* 徙錢 to waste money

sāaisí 徙士 size

sāam 三 three

sāam-sahp 三十 thirty

sāamfahnjī-yāt 三分之一 third (1/3)

sāamgok-fu 三角褲 briefs

sāamgok-yìhng 三角形 triangle

Sāam-yuht 三月 March

sāam'kwàhn 衫裙 dress, frock

sāan 山 hill, mountain

sāanbō 山坡 slope

sāandĕng* 山頂 summit, peak

sāan'gūk 山谷 valley

sāanyèuhng 山羊 goat

sāan 閂 to turn off, shut

sāan-màaih 閂埋 to shut

sāan-mùhn 閂門 closed (door/shop)

sāang 生 to give birth

sāang ge 生嘅 raw, uncooked, rare

sāang(máahng) 生猛 alive

sāangbóu-yàhn 生埠人 stranger

sāangchāu 生抽 soy sauce (salty)

sāanggwó 生果 fruit

sāangyaht 生日 birthday

Sāangyaht Faailohk 生日快樂 Happy Birthday!

sāanwùh 珊瑚 coral

sáanjōng 散裝 loose (not in packet)

sáan'ngán*/án* 散銀 change, small

saat 殺 kill, murder

saatjai 剎掣 brake, to brake

saatnàhgāan 剎那間 moment (instant)

sáauwàih 稍為 slightly

sāibāk 西北 north-west

sāi'bīn/bihn 西邊 west

sāigwā 西瓜 watermelon

Sāifōng-yàhn 西方人 Westerner

sāijōng 西裝 suit, business

sāikāhn 西芹 celery

sāilàahnfā-choi 西蘭花菜 broccoli

sāi'nàahm/làahm 西南 south-west

sái 洗 to wash

sáichín* 洗錢 to spend

sáisáu-gāan 洗手間 toilet

sáigit-jīng 洗潔精 detergent

sáitàuh-sēui 洗頭水 shampoo

sáiwún 洗碗 to wash the dishes

sai 細 little, young

saichèuhng 細長 slender

saihā 細蝦 shrimp, prawn

sai-lèuihgwún 細旅館 lodge, small hotel

sailōu 細佬 brother (younger)

saimānjái 細蚊仔 child (young person)

saisíu 細小 tiny

saigaai 世界 world

saigéi 世紀 century

sāk 塞 plug (bath)

sām 深 deep

sāmjohng 心臟 heart

sāmpóuh 心抱 daughter-in-law

31

S

sāmlàhm 森林 forest

sám 嬸 aunt (wife of father's younger brother)

sānchíng 申請 to apply (for permission)

sāntái 身體 body

sān'gōu 身高 height (body)

sān 新 new

Sān'gabō 新加坡 Singapore

Sān'gabō ge 新加坡嘅 Singaporean (in general)

Sān'gabō-yàhn 新加坡人 Singaporean (people)

sānlòhng 新郎 bridegroom

sānmán* 新聞 news

sānmàhn-gaai 新聞界 press, journalism

sān'nèuhng/lèuhng 新娘 bride

Sānsāilàahn 新西蘭 New Zealand

Sānsāilàahn-yàhn 新西蘭人 New Zealander

sānsīn 新鮮 fresh

sānséui 薪水 salary

sàhn 神 god

Sàhndouh 神道 Shinto

sàhnfuh 神父 priest (Catholic)

sàhnsing 神聖 holy, sacred

sàhnwá* 神話 myth

sàhnlāu 晨樓 dressing gown

sahn 腎 kidney

sāngcháan 生產 to produce

sāngchyùhn 生存 to survive

sāngmihng 生命 life

sāng'wuht 生活 life

sāp 濕 wet

sahp 十 ten

sahp-baat 十八 eighteen

sahp-chāt 十七 seventeen

sahp-gáu 十九 nineteen

sahp-luhk 十六 sixteen

sahp-ńgh 十五 fifteen

sahp-sei 十四 fourteen

sahp-yāt 十一 eleven

Sahp-yāt-yuht 十一月 November

sahp-yih 十二 twelve

Sahp-yih-yuht 十二月 December

sahp-yīk 十億 billion

Sahp-yuht 十月 October

sahpjih-louhháu 十字路口 crossroads, intersection

sahpmaahn 十萬 hundred thousand

sāttàuhgō 膝頭哥 knee

sātbaaih 失敗 to fail, failure

sātjūng 失踪 missing (lost person)

sātmaht yihnglīhng-chyu 失物認領處 lost property

sātmohng 失望 disappointed

sātyihp 失業 unemployed

sāu-chín* 收錢 to collect payment

sāu-dóu* 收到 to receive

sāu-fai 收費 rate, tariff, fee

sāugeui 收據 receipt

sāujaahp 收集 to gather

sāu-màaih 收埋 hidden

sāusahp 收拾 tidy up

sāuyām-gēi 收音機 radio

sāubōu 修補 to mend

sāuléih 修理 to repair

sāuchí 羞恥 shame, disgrace

sáu 手 hand

sáubei 手臂 arm

sáubīu 手錶 wristwatch

sáugūng'ngaih/aih 手工藝 crafts, handicraft

sáujāang 手踭 elbow

sáují 手指 finger

sáujuhk 手續 formalities

sáu'ngáak/áak 手鈪 bracelet

sáusīk 手飾 jewelry

sáutàih-dihnwá* 手提電話 mobile phone

sáutēui-chē 手推車 cart (pushcart)

sáuwún 手腕 wrist

sáujāai 守齋 to fast

sau 瘦 thin (of persons)

saufā ge 繡花嘅 embroidered

sàuhhahn 仇恨 hatred

sauh-wāihip 受威脅 threatened
sauhfú 受苦 to suffer
sauhsēung 受傷 injured
sauhfo-yùhn 售貨員 sales assistant
sé 寫 to write
séjih-làuh 寫字樓 office
séjok 寫作 composition, writings
sèh 蛇 snake
séi 死 to die
séifó 死火 to stall (car)
séi-gēi 死機 crashed (computer)
séimòhng 死亡 death
sei 四 four
sei-sahp 四十 forty
Sei-yuht 四月 April
seifahnjī-yāt 四分之一 quarter
sek 喫 to kiss
sehktàuh 石頭 rock, stone
sēng (yām) 聲（音） sound, noise, voice
sēng 醒 awake, to wake up
sēuiyìhn 雖然 although
sēuiyiu 需要 need, to need
sēui 水 water
sēuijam 水浸 flooding
sēuijūk 水 JUG pitcher, jug
sēui'ngàuh/àuh 水牛 water buffalo
sēuitúng 水桶 bucket
seui 歲 years old
seuipín* 碎片 piece, portion, section
sèuihjihk 垂直 vertical
seuihfóng* 睡房 bedroom
seuihyī 睡衣 pyjamas
sēunmahn-chyu 詢問處 information desk
seun 信 letter
seunfūng 信封 envelope
seunsām 信心 confidence
seunsīk 信息 information
seunyahm 信任 to trust
seunyéuhng 信仰 belief, faith

seunyuhng-kāat 信用卡 credit card
sèuhn 純 pure
sèuhn 馴 tame
seuhnbín* mahn yāt geui 順便問一句 by the way
seuhn-jyuh 順住 to follow along
seuhnleih 順利 smooth (unproblematic)
seuhnlouh baaifóng 順路拜訪 stop by, to pay a visit
sēung 箱 box
sēungfūng 傷風 cold, flu
sēungháu 傷口 wound, cut (injury)
sēunghoih 傷害 injury, to hurt (cause pain)
sēungchíh 相似 to resemble, similar
sēungdōng 相當 quite (fairly)
sēungfáan 相反 opposite (contrary)
sēunggaak 相隔 apart
sēungseun 相信 to believe
sēungsīk 相識 acquaintance
sēungtùhng 相同 identical, alike
sēunghóng* 商行 firm, company
sēungyàhn 商人 businessperson
sēungyihp 商業 business
sēungpúih 雙倍 double
sēung* 相 photograph
sēung 想 to think, to ponder, to desire
sēungfaat 想法 thoughts
sēungjeuhng 想象 to imagine
sèuhngsi 嘗試 to attempt
sēuhng-chē 上車 to get on (bus/train)
sēuhng-móhng 上網 surfing on the Internet
sēuhng-syùhn 上船 to get on (boat)
sēuhng-tòhng 上堂 attend classes

S

S

Seuhngdai 上帝 God

Seuhnghói 上海 Shanghai

seuhng (go) láihbaai 上（个）禮拜 last week

seuhng (go) sīngkèih 上（个）星期 last week

seuhng'ngohk/ohk 上顎 jaw, (upper)

seuhngmihn 上面 above

seuhngsīng 上升 to rise, to ascend

sēutsāam 恤衫 shirt

sīgā-chē 私家車 motor vehicle

sīyàhn 私人 private

sīséung 思想 thoughts

sīchàuh 絲綢 silk

sīdáai* 絲帶 ribbon

sī-hōi 撕開 to tear, to rip

sí 屎 feces

si 試 to try, to taste (sample)

si-meih 試味 to taste (salty, spicy)

si-sān 試身 to try on (clothes)

si-sān-sāt 試身室 fitting room

siyihm 試驗 test

sìhgaan 時間 time

sìhgaan-bíu 時間表 schedule, timetable

sìhhāk 時刻 point (in time)

sìhkèih 時期 period (of time)

síhchèuhng 市場 market

síhjan 市鎮 town

síh-jūngsām 市中心 downtown

síh'màhn 市民 citizen

sihbīng 士兵 soldier

sihchìhng 事情 matter, issue

sihgín* 事件 happening, incident

sihhohng 事項 item, individual thing

sihsaht 事實 fact

sihsīn 事先 earlier, beforehand

sihying-sāng 侍應生 waiter, waitress

sihk 食 to eat

sihk jóuchāan 食早餐 to eat breakfast

sihk máahnfaahn 食晚飯 to eat dinner

sihk ngaan/aan'jau 食晏晝 to eat lunch

sihkmaht 食物 food

sihkpóu 食譜 recipe

sihkyīn 食煙 to smoke (tobacco)

sihnmouh 羨慕 envious, envy

sīkyéung* 式樣 pattern, design

sīk 熄 to turn off

sīkmiht 熄滅 to go out (fire, candle)

sīkdong ge 適當嘅 appropriate

sīk 識 to know, to be acquainted with

sīkfong 釋放 to release

símdihn 閃電 lightning

sím'gwōng-dāng 閃光燈 flash (camera)

sīn 先 first, earlier, beforehand

sīn'kyut-tiùhgín* 先決條件 condition (pre-condition)

sīnsāang 先生 sir (term of address), Mr

sin 線 thread, line (mark)

sin 扇 fan (for cooling)

sīng 星 star

sīngkèih 星期 week

Sīngkèih-luhk 星期六 Saturday

Sīngkèih-ńgh 星期五 Friday

Sīngkèih-sāam 星期三 Wednesday

Sīngkèih-sei 星期四 Thursday

Sīngkèih-yāt 星期一 Monday

Sīngkèih-yaht 星期日 Sunday

Sīngkèih-yih 星期二 Tuesday

síng 繩 rope, string

sing 姓 surname

singbiht 性別 sex, gender

singgaak 性格 personality

sìhng 乘 times (multiplying)

sìhngbún 成本 cost

sìhnggūng 成功 success

sìhngjīk 成績 result

sìhng'wàih 成為 to become

s

sìhngyàhn 成人 adult
sìhnghaak 乘客 passenger
sìhngsaht 誠實 honest
sìhngsíh 城市 city
sìhngsíh ge 城市嘅 urban
sìhngyihng 承認 to admit, to confess
sipkahp 涉及 to involve
sipkahp-dou 涉及到 involved
sipluhk 攝錄 to videotape
sipluhk-dáai* 攝錄帶 video cassette
sipluhk-gēi 攝錄機 video recorder
sīu 燒 roast, grill, to burn
sīuhāau 燒烤 to grill
sīu-sēung 燒傷 burn (injury)
sīuhín 消遣 pastime
sīuhéui 少許 slight
sīubihn 小便 to urinate
síuhohksāang 小學生 school child
síujé 小姐 Miss
síusām 小心 cautious
síusyut 小説 novel
síutāu 小偷 pickpocket
siu 笑 to laugh, to smile
siuwá* 笑話 joke
sō 梳 comb
sōchoi 蔬菜 vegetable
sōfá* 梳化 sofa, couch
só 鎖 lock
só-jyuh 鎖住 locked
só-màaih 鎖埋 to lock
sósìh 鎖匙 key (to room)
sóyáuh 所有 possessions
sóyíh 所以 so, therefore
sokgāau 塑膠 plastic
Sōugaaklàahn 蘇格蘭 Scotland
Sōugaaklàahn ge 蘇格蘭嘅 Scottish (in general)
Sōugaaklàahn-yàhn 蘇格蘭人 Scottish, Scots
sōuyíu 騷擾 disturbance
sóu* 數 count

sóu 嫂 sister-in-law (wife of husband's older brother)
soubá 掃把 broom
soudeih 掃地 to sweep
sougeui-luhkjeuhng-gēi 數據錄像機 DVD
soujih 數字 figure, number
soumuhk 數目 amount
sousihk ge 素食嘅 vegetarian
suhk ge 熟嘅 ripe
suhklihn 熟練 skilful
suhkyàhn 熟人 to be acquainted
suhkyū 屬於 to belong to
sūk 叔 uncle (father's younger brother)
sūkjái 叔仔 brother-in-law (husband's younger brother)
sūkmáih 粟米 sweetcorn
sūng-jó 鬆咗 loose (wobbly)
sung 送 to send
sung 餸 dish (particular food)
sùhngbaai 崇拜 to worship
syū 書 book
syūgá* 書架 bookshelves
syūtói 書檯 desk
syū 輸 to lose, be defeated
syū-chín* 輸錢 to lose money
syūfuhk 舒服 comfortable
syuh 樹 tree
syuhyihp 樹葉 leaf
syūn 孫 grandchild, grandson
syūn'néui*/léui* 孫女 granddaughter
syūn 酸 sour
syúnhoih 損害 to damage
syún'géui 選舉 election
syúnjaahk 選擇 choice, to choose
syunpùhn 算盤 abacus
syuntàuh 蒜頭 garlic
syùhn 船 ship, boat
syut 雪 snow
syutgā 雪茄 cigar
syutgōu 雪糕 ice cream
syut'gwaih 雪櫃 refrigerator

T

taai 太 too (excessive)

taaitáai* 太太 madam (term of address), Mrs, wife

taaiyèuhng 太陽 sun

taaiyèuhng-yàuh 太陽油 sunscreen lotion

taaidouh 態度 attitude

Taaigwok 泰國 Thailand

Taaigwok ge 泰國嘅 Thai (in general)

Taaigwok-yàhn 泰國人 Thai (people)

Taai'mán*/màhn 泰文 Thai (language)

taaiyèung-yàuh 太陽油 sunscreen lotion

tāan 攤 stall (of vendor)

taap 塔 tower

tāi 梯 ladder

tái 睇 to look at, to see, to watch

tái-fūnggíng 睇風景 sightseeing

tái-behng 睇病 consultation (by doctor)

tái-dākmìhng 睇得明 able to understand (reading)

tái-gin 睇見 to see

tái-háh 睇吓 look!

tái-jyuh 睇住 look out!

tái-lohk 睇落 look, seem, appear

táimìhng 睇明 understood (by reading)

tái-mh'chīngchó 睇唔清楚 can't see clearly

tái-mh'gin 睇唔見 can't see

tái-mh'mìhng 睇唔明 not able to understand (by reading)

tái-syū 睇書 to read

táichúhng 體重 body weight

táiwān 體溫 temperature (body)

táiyihm 體驗 to experience

tai-sōu 剃鬚 to shave

tàih-dou 提到 to mention

tàihgōu 提高 to raise, to lift

tàihgūng 提供 offering

tàih-héi 提起 lift, raise

tàih-séng 提醒 to remind

tàihyíh 提議 suggestion, to suggest

tàihmuhk 題目 topic

tān 吞 to swallow

tāu 偷 to steal

tàuh 頭 head

tàuhfaat 頭髮 hair

tàuhgān 頭巾 headdress

tàuhtung 頭痛 headache

tàuh-piu 投票 to vote

tàuhsou 投訴 complaint

tēng 聽 to hear, to listen

tēng-dākmìhng 聽得明 able to understand (hearing)

tēng-mh'mìhng 聽唔明 not able to understand (by hearing)

tēng-mìhng 聽明 understood (by hearing)

tēng-dóu* 聽到 able to hear

tēng-jyuh 聽住 Listen!

tēng-lohkheui 聽落去 continue to listen

tēng-mh'chīngchó 聽唔清楚 can't see clearly

tēng-mh'gin 聽唔見 can't see

tēngwah 聽話 obedient

tēui 推 to push

tēuichìh 推遲 to put off, to delay

tēuijin 推薦 to recommend

téui 腿 leg

teuiyāu 退休 retired

tīsēut T恤 teeshirt

tìhm 甜 sweet (taste)

tìhmbán 甜品 sweet, dessert

tìhmsyūn 甜酸 sweet and sour

tìhmtáu* 甜頭 sweetener (incentive)

tīnfābáan 天花板 ceiling

tīnhei 天氣 weather

tīnhūng 天空 sky

Tīnjyúgaau ge 天主教嘅 Catholic (in general)

Tīnjyúgaau-tòuh 天主教徒 Catholic (people)

W

tìhnbíu 填表 fill out (form)

tīngyaht 聽日 tomorrow

tìhng 停 to stop

tipsān-dyúnfu 貼身短褲 panties

tīpsí 貼士 tip (gratuity)

tit 鐵 iron (metal)

titlouh 鐵路 railroad, railway

titsín* 鐵線 wire

tīujin 挑戰 challenge

tīusyún 挑選 to select

tīuhāk 雕刻 to carve

tīuhāk-bán 雕刻品 carving

tīusok 雕塑 to sculpt, sculpture

tiu 跳 to jump

tiumóuh 跳舞 to dance

tìuhfún 條款 item, individual thing

tìuhgín* 條件 condition (subjective/objective)

tōháai* 拖鞋 slippers

tóh'yùhn-yìhng 橢圓形 oval (shape)

tói 檯 table

tóibou 檯布 tablecloth

tokpún* 托盤 tray

tóng* 糖 candy, sweets

tongdáu 熨斗 iron (for clothing)

tongsāam 熨衫 iron, to (clothing)

tòhng 糖 sugar

tòhnggwó 糖果 confectionery

tóu* 桃 peach

tóuleuhn 討論 discussion, to discuss

tóujyu 土著 indigenous (people)

tóujyu ge 土著嘅 indigenous (in general)

tou 套 set

tòuh 圖 drawing

tòuhsyū-gwún 圖書館 library

tóuh 肚 stomach, belly

tóuh'náahm/láahm 肚腩 abdomen

tūnggwo 通過 through, past

tungjī 通知 notice, to inform

tūngsèuhng 通常 usually

tūngseun 通信 correspond (write letters)

tung 痛 sore, painful

tungfú 痛苦 suffering

tùhng 同 with, and

tùhng ... lyùhnlok 同 ... 聯絡 to contact, to get in touch with

tùhng ... sēunglèuhng 同 ... 商量 consult, talk over with

tùhngmàaih 同埋 and

tùhngsìh 同時 meanwhile

tùhngsih 同事 co-worker, colleague

tùhngyēung*-gám* 同樣咁 likewise

tùhngyi 同意 to agree

tùhng 銅 bronze, copper

tyùhntái 團體 group

tyúhn-jó 斷咗 broken, snapped (of bones, etc.)

tyut 脫 take off (clothes)

W

wá* 畫 picture, painting

wah béi ... jī 話俾 ... 知 to let someone know

waaih 壞 bad

waaih-jó 壞咗 broken, does not work, off (gone bad)

waaih-sāmchèuhng ge 壞心腸 嘅 wicked

wàaihyahn 懷孕 pregnant

wàaihyìh 懷疑 to doubt, to suspect

waahk 畫 to draw

waahk-wá* 畫畫 to draw a painting

waahkjé 或者 or, maybe, perhaps

wáan 玩 to play

wàahn 還 to return, to give back

wàahnpèih 頑皮 naughty

wàahn'gu 頑固 stubborn, determined

wàahn'gíng 環境 environment, surroundings

wàahnyíu 環繞 round, around

wàahnggwo 橫過 across

waaht'syú 滑鼠 mouse (computer)

Wāiyíhsī 威爾斯 Wales

Wāiyíhsī ge 威爾斯嘅 Welsh (in general)

Wāiyíhsī-yàhn 威爾斯人 Welsh (people)

wái 喂 hello! (on phone)

wai 喂 to feed

wàihyāt 唯一 sole, only

wàihhahm 遺憾 regrettably

wáihdaaih 偉大 grand, great

waihyū 位於 to be located

waih 為 for

waih ... fuhkmouh 為 ... 服務 to serve

waih ... yuhng ge 為 ... 用嘅 intended for

wānchyùhn 溫泉 hot spring

wāndouh 溫度 temperature (heat)

wānnyúhn 溫暖 warm, warmth

wānyàuh 溫柔 gentle

wán 搵 to find

wahnduhng 運動 sports

wahnhei 運氣 luck

wahn'ngàauh/àauh 混淆 to confuse

wàhng'wáih 宏偉 great, impressive

wíhnggáu ge 永久嘅 permanent

wíhngmóuh 永冇 never

wíhng'yúhn 永遠 forever

wòh'nyúhn/lyúhn 和暖 mild (not cold)

wohk 鑊 pan

wòhngfān 黃昏 dusk

wòhnggwā 黃瓜 cucumber

wòhngsīk 黃色 yellow

wòhnggūng 皇宮 palace

wūdím 污點 stain

wūjōu 污糟 dirty

wūgau 污垢 dirt, filth

wūyīng 烏蠅 fly (insect)

wūgwāi 烏龜 turtle (land)

Wuhlyùhn-móhng 互聯網 Internet

wùh 壺 pot

wùh 湖 lake

wùhdíp* 蝴蝶 butterfly

wùhsōu 鬍鬚 moustache, beard

wùhtòuh 糊塗 confused (mentally)

wuhjiu 護照 passport

wúi*yùhn 會員 member

wùihdaap 回答 to reply (in speech)

wùihfūk 回覆 to reply (in writing)

Wùihgaau ge 回教嘅 Muslim (in general)

Wùihgaau-míu* 回教廟 mosque

Wùihgaau-tòuh 回教徒 Muslim (people)

wùihyīk 回憶 memories

wúih 會 can, be able to

wuihwá* 會話 conversation

wuihyíh 會議 meeting

wuihbou 匯報 to report

wún 碗 bowl

wuhn 換 to change, to switch

wuhn-chín* 換錢 change, exchange (money)

wuhn-sāam 換衫 to get dressed

wuhn'geuih 玩具 toy

wuhtduhng 活動 activity

Y

yáh 也 also

yáai-dāanchē 踩單車 to ride (bicycle)

yām-chàhm-chàhm 陰沉沉 dull (weather)

yāmdouh 陰道 vagina

yāmging 陰莖 penis

yāmlèuhng-deihfōng 陰涼地方 shade

yāmtīn 陰天 overcast, cloudy

yāmpui 欽佩 to admire

yām'ngohk/ohk 音樂 music

yām'ngohk/ohk-tēng 音樂廳 concert hall

yām'ngohk/ohk-wúi* 音樂會 concert

yám 飲 to drink

yám-jeui 飲醉 drunk

yámsing 飲勝 cheers!

yámyéh 飲嘢 drink, refreshment

yahmhòh-deihfōng 任何地方 anywhere

yahmhòh-sih 任何事 anything

yahmhòh-yàhn 任何人 anybody, anyone

yānchí 因此 therefore

yānwaih 因為 because

yányìhng-ngáahn/áahn'gēng* 隱形眼鏡 contact lens

Yandouh 印度 India

Yandouh ge 印度嘅 Indian (in general)

Yandouh-yàhn 印度人 Indian (people)

Yandouhnèihsāi'a 印度尼西亞 Indonesia

Yan'nèih 印尼 Indonesia

Yan'nèih ge 印尼嘅 Indonesian (in general)

Yan'nèih-yàhn 印尼人 Indonesian (people)

Yan'nèih-yúh 印尼語 Indonesian (language)

yanjeuhng 印象 to make an impression

yanjeuhng sāmhāk ge 印象深刻嘅 impressive

yàhn 人 person, people

yàhnchìhng-meih 人情味 human (feelings)

yàhnháu 人口 population

yàhnjeuhng 人像 statue

yàhnjouh ge 人造嘅 synthetic

yàhn'gūng 人工 wages

yàhn'gūng ge 人工嘅 artificial

yahp 入 enter

yahpbihn 入邊 inside

yahpháu 入口 to import, entrance, way in

yāt 一 one

yāt bouhfahn 一部份 partly

yāt chē (fomaht) 一車（貨物） load

yāt chi 一次 once

yāt dā 一打 dozen

yāt deui 一對 a pair of

yāt-fàahn-fūng-seuhn 一帆風順 bon voyage!

yāt fahn 一份 portion, serve

yāt-yìhn-wàih-dihng 一言為定 agreed!

yātbūn 一般 average (so-so, just okay)

yātbun 一半 half

yatchai 一切 everything

yātchàih 一齊 together

yātdī 一啲 a little

yātdihng 一定 must, certain, sure

yātguhng 一共 altogether, in total

yāthaih ... yāthaih 一係 ... 一係 either

yātjahn'gāan 一陣間 later

yātjahn gin 一陣見 see you later!

yātjihk heui 一直去 straight ahead

yātsai 一世 lifetime

yātyeuhng 一樣 same

Yāt-yuht 一月 January

yaht 日 day

Yahtbún 日本 Japan

Yahtbún ge 日本嘅 Japanese (in general)

Yahtbún-yàhn 日本人 Japanese (people)

yahtchēut 日出 sunrise

yahtchìhng-bíu 日程表 schedule

yahtgei 日記 diary

Y

yahtkèih 日期 date (of the month)

yahtlohk 日落 sunset

Yahtmán* 日文 Japanese (language)

yahtsèuhng 日常 daily

yāuga-yaht 休假日 day off

yāumahk 幽默 humorous

yāumahkgám* 幽默感 sense of humor

yāusau 優秀 excellent

yāusīk 休息 to rest, to relax

yáu* 油 paint

yàuhkèih-sih 尤其是 particularly, especially

yàuh 油 oil

yàuhjā 油渣 diesel oil

yàuhja 油炸 fried

yàuh'neih/leih 油膩 fatty, greasy

yàuh-yáu* 油油 to paint (house)

yàuhgúk* 郵局 post office

yàuhpiu 郵票 stamp (postage)

yàuhhaak 遊客 tourist

yàuhhei 遊戲 game

yàuhséui 游水 to swim

yàuhséui-sāam 游水衫 swimming costume

yàuhséui-chìh 游水池 swimming pool

yàuhwìhng-chìh 游泳池 swimming pool

yàuhwòh 柔和 mild (not severe)

yàuhyú* 魷魚 squid

yáuh 有 there is, there are

yáuh yàhn dá-gán 有人打緊 engaged (telephone)

yáuhcheui 有趣 interesting

yáuhchín* 有錢 well off, wealthy

yáuhduhk 有毒 poisonous

yáuhgwāan 有關 about, concerning

yáuh kāpyáhn-lihk 有吸引力 attractive

yáuhhaauh 有效 valid

yáuhjeuih 有罪 guilty (of a crime)

yáuhméng* 有名 famous

yáuhsìh 有時 sometimes, from time to time

yáuhyàhn 有人 somebody, someone

yáuhyuhng 有用 useful

yáuhsihn 友善 friendly, outgoing

yauh'bīn/bihn 右邊 right-hand side

yauh ... yauh 又 ... 又 both ... ...and

yèhchoi 椰菜 cabbage

yèhchoi-fā 椰菜花 cauliflower

yèhjí 椰子 coconut

yèhyèh-màhmàh 爺爺嫲嫲 grandparents (paternal)

yéh 嘢 object, thing

yéhsāang ge 野生嘅 wild

yeh'máahn 夜晚 at night

yèhng 贏 to win

yeukwuih 約會 appointment

yeuhk 弱 weak

yeuhk 藥 medicine

yeuhkdāan 藥單 prescription

yeuhkfòhng 藥房 pharmacy, drugstore

yeuhk'yún 藥丸 tablets, pills

yeuhnhàuh-tōng* 潤喉糖 cough lolly

yèuhng 羊 sheep

yèuhngmòuh 羊毛 wool

yèuhng'yuhk 羊肉 lamb, mutton

yèuhngchūng 洋蔥 onion

yèuhnggwōng 陽光 sunlight

yéuhngyuhk 養育 bring up (children)

yeuhngbún 樣本 sample

yī 姨 sister-in-law (wife's sister)

yī 醫 to treat (medically)

yīlìuh 醫療 medical

yīsāng 醫生 doctor

yīyún 醫院 hospital

yīfuhk 衣服 clothes, garment

Y

yīgā 依家 now
yī'kaau 依靠 to depend on
Yīsīlàahn'gaau 伊斯蘭教
  Islam
Yidaaihleih 意大利 Italy
Yidaaihleih ge 意大利嘅
  Italian (in general)
Yidaaihleih-mán* 意大利文
  Italian (language)
Yidaaihleih-yàhn 意大利人
  Italian (people)
yigin 意見 opinion, advice
yisī 意思 meaning
yisīk 意識 awareness
yihsīk-dou 意識到 to be
  conscious of
yi'ngoih/oih 意外 accident
yìh'gā 而家 now
yìhché 而且 moreover
yìhgāau 移交 hand over
yìhsām 疑心 suspicion
yìhjéung* 姨丈 uncle (husband
  of mother's sister)
yìh'mā 姨媽 aunt (wife of
  mother's older/younger sister)
yíh-fān 已婚 married
yíhgīng 已經 already
yíh-song'ngáuh/áuh 已喪偶
  widowed
yíhchìhn 以前 before (in time)
yíhhah 以下 following
yíhji 以致 in order that, so that
yíhjái 耳仔 ear
yíhwáan 耳環 earrings
yih 二 two (numeral)
yih-sahp 二十 twenty
Yih-yuht 二月 February
yīkjai 抑制 to restrain
yīk 億 hundred million
yihk m̀h'haih 亦唔係 nor
yihk 翼 wing
yìhm 嫌 to dislike
yìhm 鹽 salt
yìhmgaak 嚴格 strict
yìhmjuhng 嚴重 serious
  (severe)
yìhmlaih 嚴厲 severe

yìhmsūk 嚴肅 serious (not
  funny)
yīn 煙 smoke
yīnjái 煙仔 cigarette
yīnfā 煙花 fireworks
yínchēut 演出 performance
yín'góng 演講 speech, to
  make a speech
yinwuih 宴會 banquet
yihndoih 現代 modern
yihnfún 現款 cash, money
yihnsìh 現時 nowadays
yihnsìhng 現成 ready
yìhnhauh 然後 then
yìhnjuhk 延續 last (endure)
yìhnkèih 延期 to postpone
yìhnyúh 言語 language
yìhn'gau 研究 research
Yīngdahkmóhng 英特網
  Internet
Yīnggwok 英國 Britain/
  England/United Kingdom
Yīnggwok ge 英國嘅 British/
  English (in general)
Yīnggwok-yàhn 英國人 British
  (people), English (person)
yīngjeun 英俊 handsome
Yīngmán*/Yīngmàhn 英文
  English (language)
Yīngyúh 英語 English
  (language)
yīnggōi 應該 ought to
yīngyìh-chòhng 嬰兒床 cot
yíng 影 shadow
yínghéung 影響 to influence
yínghéung-lihk 影響力
  influence
yíngmàih 影迷 fan (of movies)
yíngséung* 影相 to
  photograph
yíngséung*-gēi 影相機
  camera
yìhngjohng 形狀 shape
yìhngsìhng 形成 to shape, to
  form
yìhngyìhn 仍然 still, even now
yihngdāk 認得 to recognize

Y

yihngwàih 認為 to reckon, to have an opinion

yihp 頁 page

yiht 熱 hot (temperature)

yīuchíng 邀請 invitation, to invite

yīukàuh 要求 to request (formally)

yiu 要 to want, to ask for

yìuh 搖 to shake

yìuhbáai 搖擺 to swing

yìuhfóng 搖晃 to shake something

yìuhsyu 饒恕 forgiveness, mercy

yūsih 於是 thus, so

yú* 魚 fish

yùhlouh 魚露 fish sauce

yúhāk 瘀黑 bruise

yùhgwó 如果 if

yùhgwó m̀h'haih 如果唔係 else: or else

yùhhòh 如何 how?

Yùhgā-sīséung 儒家思想 Confucianism

Yùhgaau 儒教 Confucianism

yúh 雨 rain

yúh ... sēungbéi 與 ... 相比 compared with, to compare

yúhfòhng 乳房 breasts

yúhjaau 乳罩 bra

yuhdehng 預訂 to reserve (ask for in advance)

yuhyeuk 預約 to fix (a time), appointment

yuhfaai 愉快 enjoyable

yuhk 肉 meat

yuhkdáu* 肉豆 bean

yuhktōng 肉湯 broth, soup

yuhkyún 肉丸 meatball

yuhkgōng 浴缸 bathtub

yuhkyī 浴衣 bathrobe

yún* 院 courtyard

yun 怨 to blame

yùhnbāt 鉛筆 pencil

yùhn'hyūn 圓圈 circle

yùhnyìhng 圓形 round (shape)

yùhnjí-bāt 原子筆 ballpoint pen

yùhnleuhng 原諒 to forgive

yùhnyān 原因 cause, reason

yùhnchyùhn 完全 completely

yùhnsìhng 完成 to finish, to complete

yùhnyàhn 猿人 ape

yúhn 遠 far

yúhn 軟 soft

yúhn'gín* 軟件 software (computer)

yuhnmohng 願望 desire

yúngyáuh 擁有 to own

yùhnghāp 融洽 harmonious

yùhnghéui 容許 be allowed to

yùhngyih 容易 simple, easy

yúhnggám 勇敢 brave, daring

yuhng 用 to use, by means of

yuhng-yùhn 用完 finished (none left)

yuhngyi 用意 to mean (intend)

yuht 月 month

yuhtgīng-kèih 月經期 period (menstrual)

yuhtleuhng 月亮 moon

yuhtgwo 越過 to go past

Yuht'nàahm/làahm 越南 Vietnam

Yuht'nàahm/làahm-wá* 越南話 Vietnamese (language)

Yuht'nàahm/làahm-yàhn 越南人 Vietnamese (people)

Yuht'nàahm/làahm ge 越南嘅 Vietnamese (in general)

English–Cantonese

A

abacus syunpùhn 算盤

abdomen tóuh'nàahm/làahm 肚腩

ability nàhng/làhng'lihk 能力

able to hóyíh 可以

able to hear tēng-dóu* 聽到

able to understand (hearing) tēng-dākmìhng 聽得明

able to understand (reading) tái-dākmìhng 睇得明

about (approximately) daaihyeuk 大約

about (regarding) yáuhgwāan 有關

above seuhngmihn 上面

abroad gwok'ngoih/oih 國外

absent kyutjihk 缺席

accept, to jipsauh 接受

accident yi'ngoih/oih 意外

accommodation jyuhsūk 住宿

accompany, to pùih 陪

according to gān'geui 根據

accuse, to jíjaak 指責

ache, to tung 痛

acquaintance sēungsīk 相識

acquainted, to be suhkkyàhn 熟人

across wàahnggwo 橫過

across from hái/héung ... deuimihn 喺/響 ... 對面

act, to jouh 做

action hàhngduhng 行動

activity wuhtduhng 活動

actually kèihsaht 其實

add, to gā 加

address deihjí 地址

admire, to yāmpui 欽佩

admit, confess sìhngyihng 承認

adult sìhngyàhn 成人

advance, go forward chìhnjeun 前進

advance money, deposit ngon/on'gām 按金

advice yigin 意見

advise, to béi ... yigin 俾 ... 意見

aeroplane fēigēi 飛機

affect, to yínghéung 影響

affection gámchìhng 感情

afford, to fuhdāam-dākhéi 負擔得起

afraid pa 怕

after jīhauh 之後

afternoon (3 pm to dusk) hah'ngh 下午

afternoon (midday) jūng'ngh 中午

afterwards, then hauhlòih 後來

again joi 再

age nìhn/lìhn'géi, nìhn/lìhn'lìhng 年紀 / 年齡

ago yìhchìhn 以前

agree, to tùhngyi 同意

agreed! yāt-yìhn-wàih-dihng 一言為定

agreement hipdihng 協定

air hūnghei 空氣

air conditioning hūngtìuh 空調

airmail hòhnghūng-yàauhgín* 航空郵件

airplane fēigēi 飛機

airport fēigēi-chèuhng 飛機場

alcohol, liquor jáu 酒

alike sēungtùhng 相同

a little yātdī 一啲

a lot hóudō 好多

alive sāangmáahng 生猛

all yātchàih 一齊

alley, lane hóng* 巷

allow, permit jéunhéui 準許
allowed to yùhnghéui 容許
almost gēifùh 幾乎
alone dāanduhk 單讀
alphabet jihmóuh 字母
already yíhgīng 已經
also yáh 也
altogether, in total yātguhng 一共
although sēuiyìhn 雖然
always gīngsèuhng 經常
ambassador daaihsìh 大使
America Méihgwok 美國
American (in general) Méihgwok ge 美國嘅
American (people) Méihgwok-yàhn 美國人
among hái ... jījūng 喺 ... 之中
amount soumuhk 數目
ancestor jóusīn 祖先
ancient gúdoih 古代
and tùhngmàaih 同埋
angry faat'nāu/làu 發嬲
animal duhngmaht 動物
ankle geuk'jāahng 腳踭
annoyed gīkhei 激氣
another (different) daihyih go 第二個
another (same again) joi làih yāt go 再嚟一個
annual múih'nìhn/lìhn yāt chi 每年一次
answer, to (spoken) daap 答
answer, to (written) daapfūk 答覆
answer the phone jip-dihnwá* 接電話
answering machine làuhyìhn-gēi 留言機
antiques gúwún* 古玩
anus gōngmùhn 肛門
anybody, anyone yahmhòh-yàhn 任何人
anything yahmhòh-sih 任何事
anywhere yahmhòh-deihfōng 任何地方
ape yùhnyàhn 猿人

apart sēunggaak 相隔
apart from chèuihjó ... jī'ngoih/oih 除咗 ... 之外
apartment gūngyuh 公寓
apologize, to douhhip 道歉
apparent mìhnghín 明顯
appear, become visible chēutyihn 出現
appearance, looks yēung* 樣
apple pìhnggwó 蘋果
appliance, electrical dihnhei-yuhngbán 電器用品
apply, to (for permission) sānchíng 申請
appointment yeukwuih/yuhyeuk 約會 / 預約
approach, to (in space) jipgahn 接近
approach, to (in time) lòihlàhm 來臨
appropriate sīkdong ge 適當嘅
approximately daaihyeuk/... jóyáu* 大約/... 左右
April Sei-yuht 四月
architecture ginjūk 建築
area deihkēui 地區
argue, to ngaai/aai'(gāau) 嗌 (交)
argument jāngleuhn 爭論
arm sáubei 手臂
armchair fùhsáu-yí 扶手椅
army gwāndéui* 軍隊
around (approximately) daaihyeuk/... jóyáu* 大約 ... 左右
around (nearby) fuhgahn 附近
around (surrounding) jāuwàih 周圍
arrange, to ngōn/ōn'pàaih/chàuhbaahn 安排 / 籌辦
arrangements, planning gaiwaahk 計劃
arrival doudaaht 到達
arrive, to dou 到
art ngaih/aih'seuht 藝術
article (in newspaper/journal) màhnjēung 文章

artificial yàhn'jouh ge 人造嘅

artist ngaih/aih'seuht-gā 藝術家

ashamed, embarrassed nàahn/làahn'wàihchìhng 難為情

Asia Nga/A'jāu 亞洲

ask about, to mahn 問

ask for, to yiu 要

asleep fan-jeuhk 瞓着

assemble, gather jaahp'hahp 集合

assemble, put together chai-màaih yātchàih 砌埋一齊

assist, to bōngjoh/bōngmòhng 幫助 / 幫忙

assistance bōngmòhng/hipjoh 幫忙 / 協助

astonished gám-dou gīngkèih 感到驚奇

as well dōu haih 都係

at hái/héung 喺 / 響

at home hái/héung ngūk/ūk'kéi 喺 / 響 ... 屋企

at least héimáh/jisíu 起碼 / 至少

atmosphere, ambience heifān 氣氛

at night yehmáahn 夜晚

at once màhseuhng/jīkhāk 馬上 / 即刻

at the latest jeuichìh 最遲

attack (in war) gūnggīk 攻擊

attack (with words) pìhnggīk 評擊

attain, reach daahtdou 達到

attempt kéihtòuh 企圖

attempt, to sèuhngsi 嘗試

attend, to chāamgā 參加

attend classes sèuhng-tòhng 上堂

attitude taaidouh 態度

attract kāpyáhn 吸引

attractive yáuh-kāpyáhn-lihk 有吸引力

auction, to paakmaaih 拍賣

auctioned off paakmaaih-jó 拍賣咗

August Baat-yuht 八月

aunt (father's sister, married) gūmā 姑媽

aunt (father's sister, unmarried) gūgū 姑姑

aunt (wife of father's older brother) baak'nèuhng/lèuhng 伯娘

aunt (wife of father's younger brother) sám 嬸

aunt (wife of mother's brother) kăhmmóuh 舅母

aunt (wife of mother's sister, married) yìhmā 姨媽

aunt (wife of mother's sister, unmarried) yī 姨

Australia Ngou/Ou'jāu 澳洲

Australian (people) Ngou/Ou'jāu- yàhn 澳洲人

Australian (in general) Ngou/Ou'jāu ge 澳洲嘅

authority (person) kyùhnwāi 權威

authority (power) kyùhnlihk 權力

automobile, car chē 車

autumn chāutīn 秋天

available (can be purchased) máaih-dākdóu* 買得到

available, to make jéunbeih-hóu 準備好

average (numbers) pìhnggwān 平均

average (so-so, just okay) yātbūn/màh'má*-déi* 一般 / 麻麻地

awake séng 醒

awake, wake up séng-jó 醒咗

awaken, wake someone up giu-séng* 叫醒

aware jīdou 知道

awareness yisīk 意識

B

baby bìhbī BB

back (part of body) buijck 背脊

B

back, rear hauhmihn 後面
back, to go fāan-heui 返去
back up, to jīchìh 支持
backward lohkkauh 落後
bad waaih 壞
bad luck m̀h'hóuwahn/ dóumùih 唔好運 / 倒霉
bag dói* 袋
baggage hàhngléih 行李
bake, to guhk 焗
bald gwōngtūk 光禿
ball bō 波
ballpoint pen yùhnjí-bāt 原子筆
banana hēungjīu 香蕉
bandage bāngdáai* 繃帶
bank (finance) ngàhn/ àhn'hòhng 銀行
bank (of river) hòh'ngohn/ohn 河岸
banquet yinwuih 宴會
bar (blocking way) jójí 阻止
bar (serving drinks) jáubā 酒吧
barber faatyìhng-sī 髮型師
barely gán'gán / gēifùh móuh 僅僅 / 幾乎冇
bargain, to góngga 講價
barren pàhnjehk ge 貧瘠嘅
base, foundation gēichó 基礎
based on gān'geui 根據
basic gēibún 基本
basis gēichó 基礎
basket láam 籃
basketball làahmkàuh 籃球
bathtub yuhkgōng 浴缸
bathe, take a bath chūnglèuhng 沖涼
bathe, swim yàuhséui 游水
bathrobe yuhkyī 浴衣
bathroom chūnglèuhng-fóng* 沖涼房
battle dá-jeung 打仗
bay hóiwāan 海灣
be, exist yáuh 有
beach hóitāan 海灘
bean yuhkdáu* 肉豆
beancurd dauhfuh 豆腐

beard wùhsōu 鬍鬚
beat (to defeat) dábaaih 打敗
beat (to strike) dá 打
beautiful (of man) lengjái 靚仔
beautiful (of woman) leng'néui*/léui* 靚女
beautiful (of things and places) leng/jeng 靚 / 正
because yānwaih 因為
become, to sìhngwàih 成為
bed chòhng 床
bedding péihpōu 被舖
bedclothes seuihyī 睡衣
bedroom seuihfóng* 睡房
bedsheet chòhngdāan 床單
beef ngàuh/àuh'yuhk 牛肉
before (in front of) hái/héung ... chìhnmihn 喺 / 響 ... 前面
before (in time) yíhchìhn 以前
beforehand, earlier jīchìhn 之前
begin, to hōichí 開始
beginning hōitàuh 開頭
behave bíuyihn 表現
behind hái/héung ... hauhmihn 喺 / 響 ... 後面
Beijing Bākgīng 北京
belief, faith seunyéuhng 信仰
believe, to sēungseun 相信
belongings chòihmaht 財物
belong to suhkyū 屬於
below hahmihn 下面
belt pèihdáai* 皮帶
beside hái/héung ... pòhngbīn 喺 / 響 ... 旁邊
besides chèuih-jó ... jī'ngoih/oih 除咗 ... 之外
best jeuihóu 最好
best wishes jūk néih/leih hóuwahn 祝你好運
better gang-hóu / hóu-dī 更好 / 好啲
better, get (be cured) hóujyún* 好轉
better, get (improve) bin-hóu / jeunbouh-jó 變好 / 進步咗

B

between hái/héung ... jīgāan 喺 / 響 ... 之間

bicycle dāanchē 單車

big daaih 大

bill dāan 單

bill, to pay màaih-dāan 埋單

billion sahp-yīk 十億

bird jéuk* 雀

birth, to give sāang 生

birthday sāangyaht 生日

biscuit (salty, cracker) hàahm-bénggōn 鹹餅乾

biscuit bénggōn 餅乾

bit (slightly) yātdī 一啲

bite, to ngáau/áau 咬

bitter fú 苦

black hāksīk 黑色

black beans dauhsih 豆豉

blame, to yuhn/gwāigau/jaakgwaai 怨 / 歸咎 / 責怪

bland dāandiuh 單調

blanket jīn 氈

bleed, to làuh'hyut 流血

blood hyut 血

blood vessel hyut'gwún 血管

blouse néuih/léuih'jōng-sēutsāam 女裝恤衫

blue làahm'sīk 藍色

board, to (boat) séuhng-syùhn 上船

board, to (bus, train) séuhng-chē 上車

boat syùhn 船

body sāntái 身體

body weight táichúhng 體重

boil, to jyú 煮

boiled jyú-gwo ge 煮過嘅

bone gwāttàuh 骨頭

bon voyage! yāt-fàahn-fūng-seuhn 一帆風順

book syū 書

bookshelves syūgá* 書架

border (between countries) bīn'gaai 邊界

border, edge bīnyùhn 邊緣

bored muhn/mòuhlìuh 悶 / 無聊

boring móuh yisī 冇意思

born, to be chēutsai 出世

borrow, to je 借 、

boss lóuhbáan 老闆

botanic gardens jihkmaht-yún 植物園

both léuhng (go) 兩（個）

both...and yauh ... yauh 又 ... 又

bother, disturb dágáau 打擾

bother, disturbance fàahn 煩

bottle jēun 樽

bottom (base) dái 底

bottom (buttocks) lōyáu/peigú 囉柚 / 屁股

bowl wún 碗

box sēung 箱

box (cardboard) jí'háp* 紙盒

boy nàahm/làahm'jái 男仔

boyfriend nàahm/làahm-pàhngyáuh 男朋友

bra yūhjaau 乳罩

bracelet sáu'ngáak/áak 手鈪

brain nóuh/lóuh 腦

brake, to brake saatjai 剎掣

branch (company) fānhóng* 分行

brand name mìhngpàaih 名牌

brave, daring yúhnggám 勇敢

bread mihnbāau 麵包

break, shatter dá-laahn 打爛

break apart, to ngáau/áau'tyúhn 拗斷

break down, to (car, machine) waaih-jó 壞咗

breakfast, morning meal jóuchāan 早餐

breakfast, to eat sihk-jóuchāan 食早餐

breasts yúhfòhng 乳房

bride sān'nèuhng/lèuhng 新娘

bridegroom sānlòhng 新郎

bridge kìuh 橋

brief dyúnjaahm ge / gáan'dyún ge 短暫嘅 / 簡短嘅

briefcase gūngsih-bāau 公事包

briefs sāamgok-fu 三角褲

47

B

bright gwōng 光
bring, to lō 攞
bring up (children) yéuhngyuhk 養育
bring up, to (topic) tàih-dou 提到
Britain Yīnggwok 英國
British (in general) Yīnggwok ge 英國嘅
British (people) Yīnggwok-yàhn 英國人
broad, spacious fut 闊
broadcast, program gwóngbo 廣播
broadcast, to bo-yām 播音
broccoli sāilàahnfā-choi 西蘭花菜
broken, does not work, spoiled waaih-jó 壞咗
broken, shattered dá-laahn-jó 打爛咗
broken, snapped (of bones, etc.) tyúhn-jó 斷咗
broken off fān-hōi-jó 分開咗
bronze tùhng/chīngtùhng 銅 / 青銅
broom soubá 掃把
broth, soup yuhktōng 肉湯
brother (older) gòhgō/daaihlóu 哥哥 / 大佬
brother (younger) dàihdái*/sailóu 弟弟 / 細佬
brother-in-law (husband's older brother) daaihbaak 大伯
brother-in-law (husband's younger brother) sūkjái 叔仔
brother-in-law (wife's older brother) daaihkáuh 大舅
brother-in-law (wife's older sister's husband) jéfū 姐夫
brother-in-law (wife's younger brother) káuhjái 舅仔
brother-in-law (wife's younger sister's husband) muihfū 妹夫
brown (coffee color) jyūgūlīk-sīk 朱古力色

bruise yūhāk 瘀黑
brush cháat* 刷
brush, to chaat 刷
bucket sēuitūng 水桶
Buddhism Fahtgaau 佛教
Buddhist (in general) Fahtgaau ge 佛教嘅
Buddhist (people) Fahtgaau-tòuh 佛教徒
buffalo (water buffalo) sēui'ngàuh/àuh 水牛
build, to héi (ngūk/ūk) 起 (屋)
building daaihhah 大廈
burn (injury) sīu-sēung 燒傷
burn, to sīu 燒
burned down, out sīu-taap-jó 燒塌咗
Burma Míhndihn 緬甸
Burmese (in general) Míhndihn ge 緬甸嘅
Burmese (people) Míhndihn-yàhn 緬甸人
bus bāsí 巴士
bus stop bāsí-jaahm 巴士站
business sēungyihp 商業
businessperson sēungyàhn 商人
busy (crowded) bīk(yàhn) 逼 (人)
busy (doing something) mòhng 忙
but daahnhaih 但係
butter ngàuh/àuh'yàuh 牛油
butterfly wùhdíp* 蝴蝶
buttocks peigú/lóyáu 屁股 / 囉柚
buy, to máaih 買
by means of yuhng 用
by the way seuhnbín* mahn yāt geui 順便問一句

C

cabbage yèhchoi 椰菜
cabbage, Chinese baakchoi 白菜
cake, pastry daahn'gōu 蛋糕

C

calculate gaisou 計數

calculator gaissou-gēi 計數機

call, summon jiuhgin 召見

call on the telephone dá-dihnwá* 打電話

called, named giujouh 叫做

calm pìhngjihng 平靜

Cambodia Gōumìhn/Gáanpòuhjaaih 高棉 / 柬埔寨

Cambodian (in general) Gōumìhn ge / Gáanpòuhjaaih ge 高棉嘅 / 柬埔寨嘅

Cambodian (people) Gōumìhn-yàhn/Gáanpòuhjaaih-yàhn 高棉人 / 柬埔寨人

camera yíngséung*-gēi 影相機

can, be able to wúih 會

can, may hóyíh 可以

can, tin gwuntáu* 罐頭

cancel chéuisīu 取消

candle laahpjūk 臘燭

candy, sweets tóng* 糖

can't see tái-m̀h'gin 睇唔見

can't see clearly tái-m̀h'chīngchó 睇唔清楚

Cantonese (in general) Gwóngdūng ge 廣東嘅

Cantonese (language) Gwóngdūng-wá* 廣東話

Cantonese (people) Gwóngdūng-yàhn 廣東人

capable of, to be yáuh nàhng/làhng'lihk ... 有能力 ...

capture, to jūk-dóu* 捉到

car, automobile chē 車

cardboard ngaahng/aahng'jí-bán 硬紙板

cards, game pēpáai* PAIR 牌

care for, love ngoi/oi'wuh 愛護

care of, to take jiugu 照顧

careful! síusām 小心

carpet deihjīn 地氈

carrot hùhng-lòhbaahk 紅蘿蔔

carry, to daai/lō 帶 / 攞

cart (horsecart) mǎhchē 馬車

cart (pushcart) sáutēui-chē 手推車

carve, to tīuhāk 雕刻

carving tīuhāk-bán 雕刻品

cash, money yihnfún 現款

cash a check, to deuiyihn 兌現

cassette hahpsīk-luhkyāmdáai* 盒式錄音帶

cat māau 貓

catch, to jūk-jyuh 捉住

Catholic (in general) Tīnjyúgaau ge 天主教嘅

Catholic (people) Tīnjyúgaau-tòuh 天主教徒

cauliflower yèhchoi-fā 椰菜花

cause yùhnyān 原因

cautious síusām 小心

cave ngàahm/àahm'duhng 岩洞

CD (compact disc) (gwōng) díp* (光）碟

CD-ROM gwōngpún*-yuhtduhk-hei 光盤閱讀器

ceiling tīnfābáan 天花板

celebrate, to hingjūk 慶祝

celery sāikàhn 西芹

center (of city) síh-jūngsām 市中心

center, middle jūnggāan 中間

central jūngyēung 中央

century saigéi 世紀

ceremony dínláih 典禮

certain, sure yātdihng 一定

certainly! dōngyìhn hóyíh 當然可以

certificate jingsyū 証書

chair dang 凳

challenge tīujin 挑戰

champion gwun'gwān 冠軍

chance, opportunity gēiwuih 機會

chance, by ngáuh/áuh'yìhn 偶然

change, small sáan'ngán/án 散銀

change, to (bus/train) jyunchē 轉車

change, to (conditions, situations) góibin 改變

change, exchange (money) deuiwuhn/wuhn-chín* 兌換 / 換錢

change, switch (clothes) wuhn 換

change one's mind góibin jyúyi 改變主意

character (Chinese) Honjih/ Jūngmàhn-jih 漢字 / 中文字

character (personality) singgaak 性格

characteristic dahkdím 特點

chase, to jēui 追

chase away, chase out gónchēut 趕出

cheap pèhng 平

cheat, someone who cheats pinjí 騙子

cheat, to ngāk/āk(yàhn) 呃 （人）

check, verify gímchàh 檢查

checked (pattern) gaakjái 格仔

cheek mihnjyūdān 面珠墩

cheers! yámsing 飲勝

cheese jīsí 芝士

chess gwokjai-jeuhngkéi* 國際象棋

chest (box) sēung 箱

chest (breast) hūng 胸

chew, to jiuh 嚼

chicken gāi 雞

child (offspring) jái'néui*/léui* 仔女

child (young person) saimānjái 細蚊仔

chilli pepper laahtjīu 辣椒

chilli sauce laahtjīu-jeung 辣椒醬

chilled gāpdung 急凍

chin hahpàh 下扒

China Jūnggwok 中國

Chinese (in general) Jūnggwok ge 中國嘅

Chinese (language) Jūngmán*/ Jūngmàhn 中文

Chinese (people) Jūnggwok-yàhn 中國人

Chinese chess jeuhngkéi* 象棋

chocolate jyūgūlīk 朱古力

choice, to choose syúnjaahk 選擇

chopsticks faaijí 筷子

Christian Gēidūk-tòuh 基督徒

Christianity Gēidūk-gaau 基督教

church gaautòhng 教堂

cigar syutgā 雪茄

cigarette yīnjái 煙仔

cinema heiyún 戲院

circle yùhn'hyūn 圓圈

circle (theater seats) làuhtēng 樓廳

citizen sīhmàhn/gūngmàhn 市民 / 公民

citrus cháang-gām-leuih 橙柑類

city sìhngsíh 城市

class, category júngleuih 種類

clean gōnjehng 乾淨

clean, to jíng-gōnjehng 整乾淨

cleanliness gitjihng 潔淨

clear (of weather) hóutīn 好天

clever chūngmìhng 聰明

climate heihauh 氣候

climb onto pàh-séuhng 爬上

climb up (hills, mountains) pāandāng 攀登

clock jūng 鐘

close to, nearby kāhn/ kaaugahn 近 / 靠近

close together, tight kaaugán 靠緊

close, to cover hahp-màaih 合埋

closed (door/shop) sāan-mùhn 閂門

closed (road) fūngsó-jó 封鎖咗

cloth bou 布

clothes, clothing yīfuhk 衣服

cloudy, overcast dōwàhn 多雲

cloves faahn 瓣

coat, jacket ngoih/oih'yī 外衣

coat, overcoat daaihlāu 大樓

coconut yèhjí 椰子

coffee gafē 咖啡

coin ngán*jái / sáan'ngán* 銀仔 / 散銀

cold láahng 冷

cold, flu sēungfūng 傷風

colleague, co-worker tùhngsih 同事

collect payment, to sāu-chín* 收錢

collision, to collide johng 撞

color ngàahn/àahn'sīk 顏色

comb sō 梳

combine sounds into syllables pingyām 拼音

come, to làih 嚟

come back fāan-làih 返嚟

come in yahp-làih 入嚟

come on, let's go faai-dī lā 快啲啦！

comfortable syūfuhk 舒服

command, order mihnglihng 命令

command, to jífāi 指揮

common, frequent póutūng 普通

company, firm gūngsī 公司

compared with, to compare bēigaau 比較

compete, to gingjāng 兢爭

competition bēichoi 比賽

complain, to póuh'yun 抱怨

complaint tàuhsou 投訴

complete (finished) gitchūk 結束

complete (thorough) chitdái 徹底

complete (whole) chyùhnbouh 全部

complete, to yùhnsìhng 完成

completely yùhnchyùhn/chitdái 完全 / 徹底

complicated fūkjaahp 複雜

co-worker, colleague tùhngsih 同事

composition, writings jokmán*/sējok 作文 / 寫作

compulsory kéuhngjaising ge 強制性嘅

computer dihn'nóuh/lóuh 電腦

computer (main) jyúgēi 主機

concentrate, to jaahpjūng 集中

concerning yáuhgwāan/gwāanyú 有關 / 關於

concert yām'ngohk/ohk-wúi* 音樂會

concert hall yām'ngohk/ohk-tēng 音樂廳

condensed milk lihn'náai/láai 煉奶

condition (pre-condition) sīn'kyut-tiuhgín* 先決條決

condition (status) johngfong 狀況

condition (subjective/objective) tiuhgín* 條件

condom beihyahn-tou 避孕套

confectionery tòhnggwó 糖果

confidence seunsām 信心

confidence, to have yáuh seunsām 有信心

confirm kokyihng 確認

Confucianism Yùhgā-sīséung 儒家思想

confuse, to wahn'ngàauh/àauh 混淆

confused (in a mess) lyuhn-chāt baat-jōu 亂七八糟

confused (mentally) wùhtòuh 糊塗

confusing lyuhn 亂

congratulations! gūnghéi néih/léih 恭喜你

connect together, to lìhnjip 連接

connection (transport) lìhnjip-dím/jūngjyún-jaahm 連接點 / 中轉站

conscious of, to be yihsīk-dou 意識到

consider (to have an opinion) yihng'wàih 認為

consider (to think over) háauleuih 考慮

constipation bihnbei 便秘

consulate lìhngsih-gwún 領事館

consult, talk over with tùhng ... sēunglèuhng 同 ... 商量

consultation (by doctor) tái-behng 睇病

contact, connection lyùhnlok 聯絡

contact, get in touch with tùhng ... lyùhnlok 同 ... 聯絡

contact lens yányìhng-ngáahn/áahn'géng* 隱型眼鏡

contagious chyùhnyíhm 傳染

continent jāu/daaihluhk 洲 / 大陸

continue, to gaijuhk 繼續

contraceptive pill beihyahn-yún 避孕丸

contraceptive beihyahn 避孕

contract hahptùhng/kaiyeuk 合同 / 契約

convenient fōngbihn 方便

conversation wuihwá* 會話

cook, to jyúfaahn 煮飯

cook (person) chyùhsī/chèuihsī 廚師

cook (verb) jyúsung 煮餸

cooked jyú-suhk-jó 煮熟咗

cooker, stove lòuhtàuh 爐頭

cookie, sweet biscuit kūkkèih 曲奇

cooking, cuisine paangtiuh 烹調

cool lèuhngsóng 涼爽

cool, to lèuhng-yāt-lèuhng 涼一涼

copper tùhng/jítùhng 銅 / 紫銅

copy fubún 副本

copy (verb) chāau/mòuhfóng 抄 / 模仿

coral sāanwùh 珊瑚

corn, grain sūkmáih 粟米

corner goklōktáu* 角落頭

correct ngāam/jingkok 啱 / 正確

correct, to gíujing/góijing 矯正 / 改正

correspond (write letters) tūngseun 通信

corridor jáulóng* 走廊

corrupt fuhbaaih 腐敗

cosmetics fajōng-bán 化裝品

cost sìhngbún 成本

cost (expense) faiyuhng 費用

cost (price) gachìhn 價錢

costly gwai 貴

costume màhnjuhk-fuhkjōng / heifuhk 民族服裝 / 戲服

cot bíhbī-chòhng BB 床

cotton mìhnbou 棉布

cotton wool mìhnfā 棉花

couch, sofa sōfā* 梳化

cough kātsēng 咳聲

cough, to kāt 咳

cough lolly yeuhnhàuh-tōng* 潤喉糖

cough syrup kāt-yeuhksēui 咳藥水

could, might hó'nàhng/làhng 可能

count sóu* 數

count, reckon yihng'wàih 認為

counter (for paying, buying tickets) gwaihtói* 櫃檯

country (nation) gwokgā 國家

country (rural area) hēunghá* 鄉下

courtyard yúhn* 院

courtesy láihmaauh 禮貌

cover, to jē 遮

cow ngàuh/àuh'ná/lá 牛嫲

crab háaih 蟹

cracked lit-hōi-jó 裂開咗

cracker, salty biscuit hàahm-bēnggōn 鹹餅乾

crafts sáugūng'ngaih/aih 手工藝

craftsperson gūngjeuhng 工匠

crashed (car) johng-chē 撞車

crashed (computer) séi-gēi 死機

crazy fūngkwòhng 瘋狂

create, to chongjok/chongjouh 創作 / 創造

credit card seunyuhng-kāat 信用卡

criminal jeuihfáan* 罪犯

cross, angry gīkhei 激氣

cross, go over gwo 過

crossroads sahpjih-louhháu 十字路口

crowded bīk 逼

cruel chàahnyán 殘忍

cry, to haam 喊

cry out, to daaihsēng giu 大聲叫

cry giuhaam-sēng 叫喊聲

cucumber wòhnggwā 黃瓜

cuisine, style of cooking fūngmeih-choi 風味菜

culture màhnfa 文化

cup būi 杯

cupboard būi'gwaih 杯櫃

cure (medical) jihlìuh/yī 治療 / 醫

cured, preserved gāgūng chyúhlēih 加工處理

currency chìhnbaih 錢幣

curtain chēunglím 窗簾

custom, tradition jaahpjuhk 習俗

cut (injury) sēunghháu 傷口

cut, to chit/got 切 / 割

cute, appealing hó'ngoi/oi 可愛

D

daily yahtsèuhng 日常

damage powaaih 破壞

damage, to jíngwaaih / syúnhoih 整壞 / 損害

damp chìuhsāp 潮濕

dance móuhwúi* 舞會

dance, to tiumóuh 跳舞

danger, dangerous ngàih/ àih'hím 危險

dark ngam/am 暗

date (of the month) yahtkèih 日期

date of birth chēutsāng yahtkèih 出生日期

daughter néui*/léui* 女

daughter-in-law sāmpóuh 心抱

dawn làihmìhng 黎明

day yaht 日

day after tomorrow hauhyaht 後日

day before yesterday chìhnyaht 前日

daydream, to faat-baahkyaht-muhng 發白日夢

day off yāuga-yaht 休假日

dead séi-jó 死咗

deaf lùhng 聾

death séimòhng 死亡

debt jaai 債

deceive, to hēipin 欺騙

December Sahp-yih-yuht 十二月

decision, to decide kyutdihng 決定

decline (refuse) kéuihjyuht 拒絕

decorate, to jōngsīk 裝飾

decrease, to gáamsíu 減少

deep sām 深

defeat, to dábaaih 打敗

defecate, to daaihbihn 大便

defect kyutdím 缺點

defend (in war) bóuwaih 保衛

defend (with words) bihnwuh 辯護

definite mìhngkok ge 明確嘅

degree, level chìhngdouh 程度

degrees (temperature) douh 度

delay, to dāam'ngh 耽誤

delayed (train, bus etc) máahndím 晚點

delicious hóusihk 好食

deliver, to daihsung 遞送

demand, to yīukàauh 要求
depart, to lèihhōi 離開
department bouhmùhn 部門
department store baakfo-
  gūngsī 百貨公司
departure chēutfaat 出發
depend on, to yī'kaau 依靠
deposit (leave behind with
  someone) chyùhnfong 存放
deposit (put money in the bank)
  chyùhnfún 存款
descendant hauhyeuih 後裔
describe, to mìuhsé 描寫
desert (arid land) sā'mohk 沙
  漠
desert, to abandon pāauhei 拋
  棄
desire yuhnmohng 願望
desire, to séung 想
desk syūtói 書檯
dessert tìhmbán 甜品
destination muhkdīkdeih 目的
  地
destroy, to powaaih 破壞
destroyed, ruined chēuiwái 摧
  毀
detergent sáigit-jīng 洗潔精
determined, stubborn gīn'kyut
  堅決
develop, to (film) chūngsái 沖
  洗
development, to develop
  faatjín 發展
diagonal deuigok-sin 對角線
diagonally deuigok 對角
dial, to (telephone) dá-dihnwá*
  打電話
dialect fōngyìhn 方言
diamond jyunsehk 鑽石
diary yahtgei 日記
dictionary chìhdín/jihdín 詞
  典/字典
die, to séi 死
difference (discrepancy in
  figures) chābiht 差別
difference (in quality) chāyih
  差異

different, other m̀h'tùhng 唔同
difficult kwan'nàahn/làahn 困
  難
dinner, evening meal
  máahnfaahn 晚飯
dinner, to eat sihk-máahnfaahn
  食晚飯
direction fōngheung 方向
director (of company) dúngsih-
  jéung 董事長
dirt, filth wūgau 污垢
dirty wūjōu 污糟
disappointed sātmohng 失望
disaster jōi'naahn/laahn 災難
discount gáam-ga 減價
discover, to faatyihn 發現
discussion, to discuss
  tóuleuhn 討論
disease jahtbehng 疾病
diesel oil yàuhjā 油渣
disgusting lihng yàhn
  jok'ngáu/áu 令人作嘔
dish (particular food) sung 餸
dish, platter dihp 碟
diskette chìhdíp* 磁碟
dislike, to yìhm/hìhm 嫌
display, to display chàhnliht
  陳列
dispute dáufān 糾紛
distance kéuihlèih 距離
disturb, to dágáau 打擾
disturbance sōuyíu 騷擾
divide, split up fānhōi 分開
divided by chèuih 除
divorce, to lèih-fān 離婚
divorced lèih-jó-fān 離咗婚
do, perform an action jouh
  做
don't! m̀h'hóu 唔好
don't mention it! m̀h'hóu
  haakhei 唔好客氣
do one's best jeuhn só'nàhng/
  làhng 盡所能
doctor yīsāng 醫生
document, letter màhn'gín*
  文件
dog gáu 狗

done (cooked) jyú-suhk-jó 煮
熟咗

done (finished) jouh-hóu-jó 做
好咗

door mùhn 門

double sēungpúih 雙倍

doubt, to wàaihyìh 懷疑

down, downward heung hah
向下

downstairs làuhhah 樓下

downtown sīh-jūngsām 市中
心

dozen yāt dā 一打

draw, to waahk 畫

drawer gwaihtúng 櫃桶

drawing tòuh 圖

dream muhng 夢

dream, to faat-muhng 發夢

dress, frock sāam'kwàhn 衫裙

dressed, to get wuhnsāam 換
衫

dressing gown sàhnlāu 晨褸

drink, refreshment yámyéh 飲
嘢

drink, to yám 飲

drive, to (a car) hōi-chē 開車

drought hōhnjōi 旱災

drown, to jahm-séi 浸死

drug (medicine) yeuhk 藥

drug (recreational) duhkbán 毒
品

drugstore, pharmacy
yeuhkfòhng 藥房

drunk yám-jeui 飲醉

dry gōn 乾

dry (weather) gōnchou 乾燥

dry, to chēui-gōn 吹乾

dry out (in the sun) lohng-gōn
晾乾

duck ngaap/aap 鴨

dull (boring) muhn 悶

dull (weather) yām-chàhm-
chàhm 陰沉沉

dumpling gáaují 餃子

during hái/héung ... kèihgāan
喺/響 ... 期間

dusk wòhngfān 黃昏

dust fūichàhn 灰塵

duty (import tax) gwāanseui
關稅

duty (responsibility) jaakyahm
責任

DVD sougeui-luhkjeuhng-gēi
數據錄像機

E

each, every múih 每

ear yíhjái 耳仔

earrings yíhwáan 耳環

earlier, beforehand sihsīn 事
先

early jóu 早

early in the morning jīujóu 朝
早

earn, to jaahn 賺

earth, soil nàih/làih'tóu 泥土

Earth, the world deihkàuh 地球

earthquake deihjan 地震

east dūng'bīn/bihn 東邊

easy yùhngyih 容易

eat, to sihk 食

eat breakfast sihk-jóuchāan
食早餐

eat dinner sihk-máahnfaahn
食晚飯

eat lunch sihk-ngaan/aan'jau
食晏晝

economical gīngjai sahtwaih
經濟實惠

economy gīngjai 經濟

edge bīnyùhn 邊緣

education, to educate
gaauyuhk 教育

effect, result haauhgwó 效果

effort nóuh/lóuh'lihk 努力

effort, to make an jeuhnlihk
盡力

egg gāidáan* 雞蛋

eggplant, aubergine ngái/
ái'gwā 矮瓜

eight baat 八

eighteen sahp-baat 十八

eighty baat-sahp 八十

E

either yāthaih ... yāthaih 一係 ... 一係

elbow sáujāang 手踭

elder nìhn/lìhn'géi daaih-dī ge / jéungbui 年紀大啲嘅 / 長輩

election syún'géui 選舉

electric dihnduhng ge 電動嘅

electricity dihnlàuh 電流

electronic dihnjí 電子

elegant gōu'ngáh/áh 高雅

elephant daaihbahnjeuhng 大笨象

elevator dihntāi 電梯

eleven sahp-yāt 十一

else: anything else daihyih dī 第二啲

else: or else yùhgwó m̀h'haih / fáujāk 如果唔係 / 否則

email (message) dihnjí-yàuhgín* 電子郵件

email, to faat-dihnjí-yàuhgín* 發電子郵件

email address dihnjí-yàuhgín* deihjí 電子郵件地址

embarrassed nàahn/làahn'wàihchìhng 難為情

embarrassing lihng yàhn wàih'nàahn/làahn 令人為難

embassy daaihsíh-gwún 大使館

embrace, to láam-jyuh 攬住

embroidered saufā ge 繡花嘅

embroidery chisau 刺繡

emergency gāpchán 急診

emotion chìhngséuih 情緒

empty hūng ge 空嘅

end (tip) jīm'dyūn 尖端

end (finish) jūngjí 終止

end, to gitchūk 結束

enemy dihkyàhn 敵人

energy jīnglihk 精力

engaged (telephone) yáuh yàhn góng-gán (dihnwá*) 有人講緊（電話）

engaged (to be married) dihng-fān 訂婚

engine mōdá 摩打

England Yīnggwok 英國

English (in general) Yīnggwok ge 英國嘅

English (language) Yīngmán*/Yīngmàhn/Yīngyúh 英文 / 英語

English (person) Yīnggwok-yàhn 英國人

engrave, to hāksēuhng 刻上

enjoy, to héungsauh 享受

enjoyable yuhfaai ge 愉快嘅

enjoy oneself, to gwo-dāk yuhfaai 過得愉快

enlarge, to fong-daaih 放大

enough jūkgau 足夠

enquire, to mahn 問

enter, to yahp-làih 入嚟

entirety, whole chyùhnbouh 全部

entrance, way in yahpháu 入口

envelope seunfūng 信封

envious, envy sihnmouh 羨慕

environment, the wàahn'gíng 環境

equal, equality pìhngdáng 平等

error cho'ngh 錯誤

escalator dihnduhng-làuhtāi 電動樓梯

especially yàuhkèihsih 尤其是

establish, set up ginlaahp 建立

Europe Ngāu/āu'jāu 歐洲

even (also) lìhn 連

even (smooth) pìhngwaaht 平滑

evening yehmáahn 夜晚

event sihgín* 事件

ever, have already chàhnggīng 曾經

every múih 每

everybody, everyone múih go yàhn 每个人

every kind of gok-sīk gok-yeuhng 各式各樣

everything yatchai 一切

every time múih chi 每次
everywhere dou'chyu 到處
exact, exactly koksaht 確實
exactly! just so! móuhcho 冇錯
exam, test háau-síh 考試
examine, to gímchàh 檢查
example laihjí 例子
example, for laihyùh/peiyùh
例如 / 譬如
excellent yāusau ge 優秀嘅
except chèuih-jó ... jî'ngoih/oih
除咗 ... 之外
exchange, to (money, opinions)
deuiwuhn 兌換
exchange rate deuiwuhn-léut*
兌換率
excited gám-dou hīngfáhn 感
到興奮
exciting lihng yàhn hīngfáhn
令人興奮
excuse me! (apology)
deui'mh'jyuh 對唔住
excuse me! (attracting
attention) chéng/chíng'mahn
請問
excuse me! (getting past)
mh'gōi jeje 唔該借借
exist, to chyùhnjoih 存在
exit, way out chēutháu 出口
expand, grow larger
pàahngjeung 膨漲
expect, to kèihmohng 期望
expenses faiyuhng 費用
expensive gwai 貴
experience gīngyihm 經驗
experience, to táiyihm/gīnglihk
體驗 / 經歷
expert jyūn'gā 專家
explain, to gáaisīk 解釋
export, to export chēutháu 出口
express, state bíusih 表示
extension (telephone) fān'gēi
分機
extra ngaahk/aahk'ngoih/oih ge
額外嘅
extremely gihk 極
eye ngáahn/áahn 眼

eyebrow ngáahn/áahn'mèih 眼
眉
eyelashes ngáahn/
áahn'mèihmòuh 眼眉毛
eyeglasses, spectacles
ngáahn/áahn'géng* 眼鏡

F

fabric, textile bouliú* 布料
face mihn 臉
face (respect) mihnjí 面子
face, to mihndeui 面對
fact sihsaht 事實
factory gūngchóng 工廠
failure, to fail sātbaaih 失敗
fake (imitation) mouhpàaih-fo/
gá*mouh ge 冒牌貨 / 假冒嘅
fall (season) chāutīn 秋天
fall, to dit-lohklàih 跌落嚟
fall over dit-dóu 跌倒
false (not true) gá* ge 假嘅
family gātìhng 家庭
famine gēifōng 飢荒
famous yáuhméng*/
chēutméng* 有名 / 出名
fan (electrical) fūngsin 風扇
fan (for cooling) sin 扇
fan (of movies) yíngmàih 影迷
fan (of music) gōmàih 歌迷
fancy kèihdahk 奇特
far yúhn 遠
fare fēi 飛
fast, rapid faai 快
fast, to sáujāai 守齋
fatty, greasy fèih/yauh'neih/
leih 肥膩 / 油膩
fat, plump fèih 肥
father bàhbā*/abā* 爸爸 / 呀爸
father-in-law ngohk/ohk'fú*,
ngoih/oih'fú* 岳父 / 外父
fault gwosāt 過失
fax, to fax chyùhnjān 傳真
fear pa 怕
February Yih-yuht 二月
fee sāufai 收費
feed, to wai 餵

F

feel, to gokdāk 覺得

feeling gámgok 感覺

female néuih/léuih'sing ge 女性嘅

fence lèihbā 籬笆

ferry douhsyùhn 渡船

fertile fèihyūk 肥沃

festival jityaht 節日

fetch, to ló 攞

fever faatsīu 發燒

few géi go 幾個

fiancée meihfān-fū 未婚夫

fiance meihfān-chāi 未婚妻

field, empty space hūngdeih 空地

fierce hūngmáahng 兇猛

fifteen sahp-ńgh 十五

fifty ńgh-sahp 五十

fight, to (physically) dágāau 打交

fight over, to jāang 爭

figure, number soujih 數字

Filipino (Tagalog) Fēileuhtbān-yúh 菲律賓語

fill, to jōngmúhn 裝滿

fill out (form) tìhnbíu 填表

film (camera) fēilám* 菲林

film, movie dihnyíng 電影

final jeui'hauh 最後

finally jūngyū 終於

find, to wán 搵

fine (okay) dāk 得

fine (punishment) fahtfún 罰款

finger sáují 手指

finish yùhnsìhng 完成

finish off, to jouh-màaih 做埋

finished (completed) jouh-yùhn 做完

finished (none left) yuhng-yùhn 用完

fire fó 火

fire someone, to cháau (kéuih) yàuhyú* 炒（佢）魷魚

fireworks yīnfā 煙花

firm (definite) gīndihng 堅定

firm (mattress) ngaahng/aahng 硬

firm, company sēunghóng* 商行

first, earlier, beforehand sīn 先

fish yú* 魚

fish, to diu-yú* 釣魚

fish sauce yùhlouh 魚露

fit, to (sái-dou) pui'hahp （使到）配合

fitting, suitable ngāamsān 啱身

fitness training gihnsān wahnduhng 健身運動

fitting room sisān-sāt 試身室

five ńgh 五

fix, to (a time, appointment) yuhyeuk 預約

fix, to (repair) sāuléih 修理

flag kèih 旗

flash (camera) sím'gwōng-dāng 閃光燈

flashlight, torch dihntúng 電筒

flavor meihdouh 味道

flat, apartment dāanwái*/gūngyuh 單位／公寓

flat, smooth pìhng 平

flight bāangēi 班機

flight number bāangēi-houh ma 班機號碼

flood hùhngséui 洪水

flooding séuijam 水浸

floor láu* 樓

flour mihnfán 麵粉

flower fā 花

flush (wash) chūngséui 沖水

fly (insect) wūyīng 烏蠅

fly, to fēi 飛

flu gámmouh 感冒

fluent làuhleih 流利

flute chèuhngdēk* 長笛

fog mouh 霧

follow along, to seuhn-jyuh 順住

follow behind, to gān-jyuh 跟住

following yíhhah 以下

fond of, to be jūngyi/héifūn 鐘意／喜歡

G

food sihkmaht 食物

foot geuk 腳

for waih 為

forbid, to gamjí 禁止

force lihkleuhng 力量

force, compel kèuhngbīk 強迫

forehead ngaahk/aahk'tàuh 額頭

foreign ngoih/oih'gwok ge 外國嘅

foreigner ngoih/oih'gwok-yàhn 外國人

forest sāmlàhm 森林

forever wìhng'yúhn 永遠

forget, to mòhnggei 忘記

forgive, to yùhnleuhng 原諒

forgiveness, mercy yìuhsyu 饒恕

forgotten mòhnggei-jó 忘記咗

fork chā 叉

form (to fill out) bíugaak 表格

formalities sáujuhk 手續

fortress bóuléuih 堡壘

fortunately hóuchói 好彩

forty sei-sahp 四十

forward heungchìhn 向前

four sei 四

fourteen sahp-sei 十四

France Faatgwok 法國

French (in general) Faatgwok ge 法國嘅

French (language) Faatmán*/Faatmàhn 法文

French (people) Faatgwok-yàhn 法國人

free, independent jihyàuh 自由

free of charge mìhnfei 免費

free of restraints mòuh-haahnjai 無限制

freedom jihyàuh 自由

freeze gitbīng 結冰

frequent gīngsèuhng 經常

fresh sānsīn 新鮮

Friday Sīngkèih-ngh/Láihbaai-ngh 星期五 / 禮拜五

fried yàuhja 油炸

friend pàhngyáuh 朋友

friendly, outgoing yáuhsihn 友善

frightened haak-chān 嚇親

from chùhng 從

front chìhnmihn 前面

front: in front of hái/héung ... chìhnmihn 喺 / 響 ... 前面

frown deui ... jau mèihtàuh 對 ... 皺眉頭

freeze (computer) séi-gēi 死機

frozen bīngdung 冰凍

fruit sāanggwó 生果

fry, to jīn 煎

fulfil yùhnsìhng 完成

full múhn 滿

full, eaten one's fill báau 飽

fun, to have wáan 玩

function, to work gūngjok 工作

funds, funding gīngfai 經費

funeral jonglaih 葬禮

funny hóusiu 好笑

furniture gāsī 傢私

further, additional jeun-yāt-bouh 進一步

fussy gwofahn jyuyi síujit 過份注意小節

future: in future jēunglòih 將來

G

gamble dóubok 賭博

game yàuhhei 遊戲

garage (for parking) chēfòhng 車房

garage (for repairs) jíngchē-chóng 整車廠

garbage laahpsaap 拉圾

garden, yard fāyún* 花園

gardens, park gūngyún* 公園

garlic syuntàuh 蒜頭

garment yīfuhk 衣服

gasoline dihnyàuh 電油

gasoline station dihnyàuh-jaahm 電油站

gate daaihmùhn 大門

G

gather, to sāujaahp 收集

gender singbiht 性別

general, all-purpose póupin 普遍

generally póupin-gám 普遍咁

generous hóngkoi 慷慨

gentle wānyàuh 溫柔

German (in general) Dākgwok ge 德國嘅

German (language) Dākmán*/ Dākmàhn 德文

German (people) Dākgwok-yàhn 德國人

Germany Dākgwok 德國

gesture jīsai 姿勢

get, receive dāk-dóu* 得到

get off (bus/train) lohk-chē 落車

get off (boat) lohk-syùhn 落船

get on (bus/train) séuhng-chē 上車

get on (boat) séuhng-syùhn 上船

get up (from bed) héisān 起身

get well soon! faai-dī hóu-fāan 快啲好番

ghost gwái 鬼

gift láihmaht 禮物

ginger gēung 薑

girl néuih/léuih'jái 女仔

girlfriend néuih/léuih-pàhngyáuh 女朋友

give, to béi 俾

given name méng* 名

glad gōuhing 高興

glass (material) bōlēi 玻璃

glass (for drinking) bōlēi-būi 玻璃杯

glasses, spectacles ngáahn/áahn'géng* 眼鏡

glutinous rice noh/loh'máih 糯米

go, to heui 去

go along, join in chāamyùh 參與

go around, visit fóngmahn 訪問

go back fāanheui 返去

go beyond chīuchēut 超出

go for a walk chēut-gāai hàhng-háh 出街行吓

go home fāan-ngūk/ūk'kéi* 返屋企

go out (fire, candle) sīkmiht 熄滅

go out, exit chēut-heui 出去

go to bed fan'gaau 瞓覺

go up, climb dāng-séuhng 登上

goal muhkdīk 目的

goat sāanyèuhng 山羊

God Seuhngdai 上帝

god sàhn 神

goddess néuih/léuih'sàhn 女神

gold gām 金

golf gōuyíhfū-kàuh 高爾夫球

good hóu 好

goodbye joigin 再見

good luck! jūk néih/léih hóuwahn 祝你好運

goose ngõ*/õ* 鵝

government jingfú 政府

gradually juhkjihm 逐漸

grand, great wáihdaaih 偉大

grandchild syūn 孫

granddaughter syūn'néui*/léui* 孫女

grandfather (maternal) ngoih/oih'gūng 外公

grandfather (paternal) ayèh 呀爺

grandmother (maternal) ngoih/oih'pòh, pòhpō* 外婆／婆婆

grandmother (paternal) a'màh 呀嫲

grandparents (maternal) gūnggūng-pòhpó* 公公婆婆

grandparents (paternal) yèhyèh-màhmàh 爺爺／嫲嫲

grandson nàahmsyūn 男孫

grapes (pòuh) tàihjí （葡）提子

grass chóu 草

grateful gámgīk 感激

grave fàhnmouh 墳墓

grey fūisīk 灰色

great, impressive wàhng'wáih 宏偉

green luhksīk 綠色

greens sōchoi 蔬菜

greet, to fūnyìhng 歡迎

greetings mahnhauh 問候

grill, to sīuhāau 燒烤

ground, earth deihmihn 地面

group tyùhntái 團體

grow, cultivate jung 種

grow larger, to jāngjéung 增長

grow up (child) jéungdaaih 長 大

Guangzhou (Canton) Gwóngjāu 廣州

guarantee bóujing 保証

guarantee, to dāambóu 担保

guard, to bóuwuh 保護

guess, to gú 估

guest haakyàhn 客人

guesthouse bān'gwún 賓館

guest of honor gwaibān 貴賓

guide, lead douhyàuh 導遊

guidebook léuihyàuh-jí'nàahm/ làahm 旅遊指南

guilty (of a crime) yáuhjeuih 有罪

guilty, to feel noih/loih'gau 內 疚

H

hair tàuhfaat 頭髮

half yātbun 一半

hall láihtòhng 禮堂

hand sáu 手

handicap bātleih-tìuhgín* 不 利條件

handicraft sáugūng'ngaih/aih 手工藝

handle beng 柄

handle, to chyúléih 處理

hand out fānfaat 分發

hand over yìhgāau 移交

handsome yīngjeun 英俊

hang, to gwa 掛

happen, occur faatsāng 發生

happened, what happened? faatsāng mātyéh sih 發生乜嘢 事

happening, incident sihgín* 事件

happy hōisām/gōuhing 開心 / 高興

Happy Birthday! Sāangyaht Faailohk 生日快樂

Happy Chinese New Year! Gūnghéi Faatchòih 恭喜發財

harbor hóigóng 海港

hard disk/drive (computer) ngaahng/aahng'pùhn 硬盤

hardly gihksíu 極少

hardworking, industrious kàhnlihk 勤力

harmonious yùhnghāp 融洽

hat móu 帽

hate, to jāng 憎

hatred sàuhhahn 仇恨

have, own yáuh 有

have been somewhere heui-gwo 去過

have done something jouh-gwo 做過

have to, must yātdihng yiu 一 定要

he, him kéuih 佢

head tàuh 頭

headache tàuhtung 頭痛

head for, toward heung-jyuh 向住

headdress tàuhgān 頭巾

healthy gihnhōng 健康

hear, to tēng 聽

heart sāmjohng 心臟

heat, to gāyiht 加熱

heavy chúhng 重

height gōudouh 高度

height (body) sān'gōu 身高

hello, hi néih/léih hóu 你好 !

hello! (on phone) wái 喂

Help! Gaumehng a! 救命啊!

help, to bōng/bōngmòhng 幫 / 幫忙

H

ENGLISH—CANTONESE

her, hers kéuih ge 佢嘅

here nī/lī'douh / nī/lī'syu 呢度 / 呢處

hidden sāu-màaih 收埋

hide, to nēi/lēi-màaih 呢埋

high gōu 高

hill sāan 山

hindrance, to hinder jó'ngoih/oih 阻礙

hire, to jōu 租

his kéuih ge 佢嘅

history lihksí 歷史

hit, strike dá 打

hobby ngoi/oi'hou 愛好

hold, to (event) géuibaahn 舉辦

hold, to (grasp) jūk-jyuh 捉住

hold back hungjai 控制

hole lūng 窿

holiday (festival) jityaht 節日

holiday (vacation) gakèih 假期

holy sàhnsing 神聖

home, house ngūk/ūk'kéi* 屋企

honest sìhngsaht 誠實

honey fūngmaht 蜂蜜

Hong Kong Hēunggóng 香港

hope, to hēimohng 希望

horse máh 馬

hospital yīyún 醫院

host jyúyàhn 主人

hot (spicy) laaht 辣

hot (temperature) yiht 熱

hotel léuihgwún 旅館

hot spring wān'chyùhn 溫泉

hour jūngtàuh 鐘頭

house ngūk/ūk 屋

how? dím/yùhhòh 點 / 如何

how are you? néih/léih hóu ma 你好嗎?

however daahnhaih 但係

how far? Géi yūhn? 幾遠?

how long? Géi chèuhng? 幾長?

how many? Géi go? 幾個?

how much? Géidō chín*? 幾多錢

how old? Géi daaih nìhn/lìhn'géi? 幾大年紀?

huge geuihyìhng 巨型

human (feelings) yàhnchìhng-meih 人情味

humid chìuhsāp 潮濕

humor yāumahk 幽默

humorous yāumahkgám 幽默感

hundred baak 百

hundred thousand sahpmaahn 十萬

hundred million yīk 億

hungry ngoh/oh 餓

hurry up! faai-dī 快啲

hurt (injured) sauhsēung 受傷

hurt, to (cause pain) sēunghoih 傷害

husband jeuhngfū 丈夫

hut, shack muhk'ngūk/ūk 木屋

I

I, me ngōh/óh 我

ice bīng 冰

ice cream syutgōu 雪糕

idea jyúyi 主意

identical sēungtùhng 相同

if yùhgwó 如果

ignore, to m̀h'léih 唔理

ignorant mòuhjī 無知

illegal fēifaat 非法

ill, sick m̀h'syūfuhk 唔舒服

illness behng 病

imagine, to séungjeuhng 想象

immediately laahphāk 立刻

impolite móuh-láihmaauh 冇禮貌

import jeunháu-fo 進口貨

import, to yahpháu 入口

importance juhngyiu-sing 重要性

important juhngyiu 重要

impossible móuh hó'nàhng/làhng 冇可能

impression, to make an yanjeuhng 印象

impressive yanjeuhng sāmhāk ge 印象深刻嘅

in, at (space) hái/héung ... yahpbihn 喺 / 響 ... 入邊

in (time, years) hái/héung 喺 / 響

in addition chí'ngoih/oih 此外

incense hēung 香

incident sihgín* 事件

included, including bāau'kwut 包括

increase, to increase jānggā 增加

indeed! góng-dāk hóu ngāam/ āam 講得好啱

indigenous (in general) tóujyu ge 土著嘅

indigenous (people) tóujyu 土著

India Yandouh 印度

Indian (in general) Yandouh ge 印度嘅

Indian (people) Yandouh-yàhn 印度人

Indonesia Yan'nèih/ Yandouhnèihsāi'a 印尼 / 印度尼西亞

Indonesian (in general) Yan'nèih ge 印尼嘅

Indonesian (language) Yan'nèih-yúh 印尼語

Indonesian (people) Yan'nèih-yàhn 印尼人

inexpensive pèhng 平

influence yínghéung-lihk 影響力

influence, to yínghéung 影響

inform, to tūngjī 通知

information seunsīk 信息

information desk sēunmahn-chyu 詢問處

inhabitant gēuimàhn 居民

inject, to jyuyahp 注入

injection dá-jām 打針

injured sauhsēung 受傷

injury sēunghoih 傷害

ink mahksēui 墨水

in order that, so that yíhji 以致

insane dīn 癲

insect chùhng 蟲

inside léuihmihn/yahpbihn 裡面 / 入邊

inside of hái/héung ... yahpbihn 喺 / 響 ... 入邊

inspect, to jímchàh 檢查

instead of doihtai 代替

instruct, tell to do something jísih 指示

insult, to insult someone mōuyuhk 侮辱

insurance bóuhím 保險

intend, to dásyun 打算

intended for waih ... yuhng ge 為 ... 用嘅

intention chyùhnsām 存心

interest (bank) leihsīk 利息

interested in gám hingcheui 感興趣

interesting (action) dākyi 得意

interesting (meaning) yáuhcheui 有趣

international gwokjai 國際

Internet Wuhlyùhn-móhng 互聯網

interpreter fāanyihk 翻譯

intersection sahpjih-louhháu 十字路口

into yahp-heui 入去

introduce oneself, to jih'ngóh/ óh gaaisiuh 自我介紹

introduce someone, to gaaisiuh 介紹

invent, to faatmìhng 發明

invitation, to invite yīuchíng 邀請

invoice fuhfún-dāan 付款單

involve, to sipkahp 涉及

involved sipkahp-dou 涉及到

Ireland Ngoi/Oi'yíhlàahn 愛爾蘭

Irish (in general) Ngoi/ Oi'yíhlàahn ge 愛爾蘭嘅

Irish (people) Ngoi/ Oi'yíhlàahn- yàhn 愛爾蘭人

ENGLISH—CANTONESE

- iron (metal) tit 鐵
- iron (for clothing) tongdáu 熨斗
- iron, to (clothing) tong 熨
Islam Yīsīlàahn'gaau / Wùihgaau 伊斯蘭教 / 回教
island dóu 島
Italian (in general) Yidaaihleih ge 意大利嘅
Italian (language) Yidaaihleih'mán*/màhn 意大利文
Italian (people) Yidaaihleih-yàhn 意大利人
Italy Yidaaihleih 意大利
item, individual thing sihhohng/ tiuhfún 事項 / 條款
ivory jeuhng'ngàh/àh 象牙

J

jacket ngoih/oih'tou 外套
jail gāamyuhk 監獄
jam gwójeung 果醬
January Yāt-yuht 一月
Japan Yahtbún 日本
Japanese (in general) Yahtbún ge 日本嘅
Japanese (language) Yaht'mán*/màhn 日文
Japanese (people) Yahtbún-yàhn 日本人
jaw, (lower) hah'ngohk/ohk 下顎
jaw, (upper) seuhng'ngohk/ohk 上顎
jealous, jealousy dougeih 妒忌
jewelry sáusīk 手飾
job gūngjok 工作
join, go along chāamgā 參加
join together, to hahp-màaih yātchàih 合埋一齊
joke siuwá* 笑話
joke, to góngsiu 講笑
journalist geijé 記者
journey louhchìhng 路程

jug, pitcher wùh 壺
juice gwójāp 果汁
July Chāt-yuht 七月
jump, to tiu 跳
June Luhk-yuht 六月
jungle chùhnglàhm 叢林
just, fair, justice gūngpìhng 公平
just, only jí(haih) 只（係）
just now ngāam'ngāam/ āam'āam 啱啱

K

keep, to bóulàuh 保留
key (computer) gihn 鍵
key (to room) sósìh 鎖匙
keyboard (of computer) gihnpùhn 鍵盤
kidney sahn 腎
kill, murder saat 殺
kilogram gūnggān 公斤
kilometer gūngléih 公里
kind, good (of persons) hóusām 好心
kind, type júngleuih 種類
king gwok'wòhng 國王
kiss máhn 味
kiss, to sek 唥
kitchen chyùh/chèuih'fóng* 廚房
knee sāttàuhgō 膝頭哥
knife dōu 刀
knock, to hāau-mùhn 敲門
know, be acquainted with sīk 識
know, be informed jīdou 知道
knowledge jisīk 知識
Korea, North Bākhòhn/ Chìuhsīn 北韓 / 朝鮮
Korea, South Nàahm/ Làahm'hòhn/Hòhn'gwok 南韓 / 韓國
Korean (language) Hòhnyúh/ Chìuhsīnyúh, 韓語 / 朝鮮語 Hòhnmàhn/Chìuhsīnmàhn 韓文 / 朝鮮文

Korean (North) Chìuhsīn-yàhn 朝鮮人

Korean (South) Hòhn'gwok-yàhn 韓國人

L

lacking kyutsíu 缺少

ladder tāi 梯

ladle, dipper chèuhngbeng-chìhgāng 長柄匙羹

lady nĕuih/leuih'sih 女仕

lake wùh 湖

lamb, mutton yèuhng'yuhk 羊肉

lamp dāng 燈

land deih 地

land, to (plane) jeuhkluhk 着陸

lane (alley) hóng* 巷

lane (of a highway) chēdouh/chēsin 車道 / 車線

language yìhnyúh 言語

Laos Lìuhgwok 寮國

Laotian Lìuhgwok-yàhn 寮國人

large daaih 大

last (endure) yìhnjuhk 延續

last (final) jeuihauh 最後

last night kàhm/chàhm'máahn 琴 / 尋晚

last week seuhng (go) sīngkèih/làihbaai 上 (个) 星期 / 禮拜

last year gauh'nín*/lín* 舊年

late (for an appointment) chìhdou 遲到

late at night ngaan/aan 晏

later gwo yātjahn'gāan 過一陣間

laugh, to siu 笑

laugh at, to chéuisiu 取笑

laws, legislation faatleuht 法律

lawyer leuhtsī 律師

layer chàhng 層

lay the table báai-tói 擺檯

lazy láahndoh 懶惰

lead (to be a leader) lìhngdouh 領導

lead (tour guide) douhyàuh 導遊

leader lĭhngdouh-yàhn 領導人

leaf syuhyihp 樹葉

leak, to lauhséui 漏水

leaded petrol hàhm'yùhn-dihnyàuh 含鉛電油

learn, to hohk 學

least (smallest amount) jeuisíu 最少

least: at least jisíu 至少

leather péi* 皮

leave, depart lèihhōi 離開

leave (train/bus) hōi-chē 開車

leave behind by accident lauh-jó 漏咗

leave behind for safekeeping làuh-chyùhn 留存

leave behind on purpose làuh-dāi 留低

lecture góngjoh 講座

lecturer (at university) góngsī 講師

left, remaining jihng-lohklàih 剩落嚟

left-hand side jó'bīn/bihn 左邊

leg téui 腿

legal hahpfaat 合法

legend chyùhn'syut 傳説

lemon, citrus nìhng/lìhng'mūng 檸檬

lemongrass hēungmàauh 香茅

lend, to je 借

length chèuhngdouh 長度

less (smaller amount) gang-síu ge 更少嘅

less, minus gáam 減

lessen, reduce gáamsíu 減少

lesson fo 課

let, allow béi 俾

let's (suggestion) ... hóu-mh-hóu a? ... 好唔好呀?

let someone know, to wah béi ... jī 話俾 ... 知

letter seun 信

level (even, flat) pìhng 平

L

level (height) gōdouh 高度

level (standard) bīujéun 標準

library tòuhsyū-gwún 圖書館

license (for driving) gasái-jāpjiu 駕駛執照

license, permit pàaihjiu/jāpjiu 牌照 / 執照

lick, to láai 舐

lid goi 蓋

lie, tell a falsehood góng-daaihwah 講大話

lie down, to fandāi 瞓低

life sāngmihng/sāng'wuht 生命 / 生活

lifetime yātsai 一世

lift (ride in car) daap-seuhnfūng-chē 搭順風車

lift, elevator dihntāi 電梯

lift, raise tàihhéi 提起

light (bright) gwōng 光

light (lamp) dāng 燈

light (not heavy) hēng 輕

lighter dáhfó-gēi 打火機

lightning símdihn 閃電

like, as hóuchíh 好似

like, be pleased by héifūn 喜歡

likewise tùhngyēung*-gám* 同樣咁

lime, citrus chēng-nìhng/lìhng'mūng 青檸檬

line (mark) sin 線

line up, to pàaih-déui* 排隊

lips jéuisèuhn 嘴唇

liquor, alcohol jáu 酒

list mìhngdāan 名單

listen, to tēng 聽

literature màhnhohk 文學

little (not much) yātdī 一啲

little (small) sai 細

live (be alive) sāang 生

live (stay in a place) jyuh 住

liver gōn 肝

load (yāt chē) fomaht (一車) 貨物

load up, to jōng-fo 裝貨

located, to be waihyū 位於

lock só 鎖

lock, to só-màaih 鎖埋

locked só-jyuh 鎖住

lodge, small hotel sai-léuihgwún 細旅館

lonely gūduhk 孤獨

long (size) chèuhng 長

long (time) noih/loih 耐

look! tái-háh 睇下

look, seem, appear tái-lohk 睇落

look after hōn'gwún 看管

look at, see tái 睇

look for wáhn 搵

look like hóuchíh 好似

look out! tái-jyuh 睇住

look up (find in book) chàh 查

loose (not in packet) sáanjōng 散裝

loose (wobbly) sūng-jó 鬆咗

lose, be defeated syū 輸

lose, mislay mh'gin-jó 唔見咗

lose money, to syū-chín* 輸錢

lose weight, to gáam-bóng*/fèih 減磅 / 減肥

lost (can't find way) màihlouh 迷路

lost (missing) sātjūng 失踪

lost property sātmaht-yìhnglíhng-chyu 失物認領處

lots of hóudō 好多

lottery chóipiu 彩票

loud daaihsēng 大聲

love ngoi/oi'chìhng 愛情

love, to ngoi/oi 愛

lovely hó'ngoi/oi 可愛

low dāi 低

luck wahnhei 運氣

lucky hahng'wahn 幸運

luggage hàhngléih 行李

lunch, midday meal nghchāan, ngaan/aan'jau 午餐 / 晏晝

lunch, to eat sihk-nghchāan, sihk-ngaan/aan'jau 食午餐, 食晏晝

lungs fai 肺

luxurious hòuhwàh 豪華

lychee laihjī 荔枝

M

Macau Ngou/Ou'mún* 澳門

machine, machinery gēihei 機器

madam (term of address) taaitáai* 太太

magazine jaahpji 雜誌

mahjong màhjeuk 麻雀

mail, post seun 信

mail, to gei 寄

main, most important jyúyiu 主要

mainly jyúyiu ge 主要嘅

major (important) juhngyiu 重要

make, to jouh 做

make do deuifuh 對付

make up, invent hēuikau/pīnjouh 虛構 / 編造

Malaysia Máhlòihsāi'nga/a 馬來西亞

Malaysian (in general) Máhlòihsāi'nga/a ge 馬來西亞嘅

Malaysian (people) Máhlòihsāi'nga/a-yàhn 馬來西亞人

male nàahm/làahm'sing 男性

man nàahm/làahm'yán* 男人

manage, succeed gwúnléih 管理

manager gīngléih 經理

Mandarin (language) Póutūng-wá*/Gwokyúh 普通話 / 國語

mango mōnggwó 芒果

manners láihmaauh 禮貌

manufacture, to jaijouh 製造

many, much hóudō 好多

map deihtòuh 地圖

March Sāam-yuht 三月

market síhchèuhng 市場

married git-jó-fān / yíhfān 結咗婚 / 已婚

marry, get married git-fān 結婚

mask mihn'geuih 面具

massage, to ngon/on'mō 按摩

mat jehk 席

match, game béichoi 比賽

matches fóchàaih 火柴

material, ingredient chòihlíu* 材料

matter, issue sihchìhng 事情

mattress chòhngyúk* 床褥

May Ńgh-yuht 五月

may hó'nàhng/làhng 可能

maybe waahkjé 或者

meal chāan 餐

mean (cruel) hākbohk 刻薄

mean (misery) gūhòhn 孤寒

mean, to (intend) yuhngyi 用意

mean, to (word) gáaisīk 解釋

meaning yisī 意思

meanwhile tùhngsìh 同時

measure, to lèuhng 量

measurements chekchyun/daaihsíu 尺寸 / 大小

measure up hahpfuh bīujéun 合符標準

meat yuhk 肉

meatball yuhk'yún 肉丸

medical yīlìuh 醫療

medicine yeuhk 藥

meet, to ginmihn 見面

meeting wuihyíh 會議

melon gwā 瓜

member wúi*yùhn 會員

memories wùihyīk 回憶

mend, to sāubóu 修補

menstruate, to làih-yuhtgīng 嚟月經

mention, to tàih-dou 提到

menu choidāan 菜單

merely gán'gán 僅僅

mess, in a lyuhn-chāt-baat-jouh 亂七八糟

message làuhyìhn 留言

metal gāmsuhk 金屬

method fōngfaat 方法

meter gūngche 公尺

meter (in taxi) bīu 表

midday jūng'ńgh 中午

middle, center jūnggāan 中間

M

middle: be in the middle of
doing dōngjūng 當中

midnight bunyeh 半夜

mild (not cold) wòh'nyūhn/
lyūhn 和暖

mild (not severe) yàuhwòh 柔
和

mild (not spicy) chīngdaahm
清淡

milk ngàuh/àuh'náaih/láaih 牛
奶

millimeter hòuhmáih 毫米

million baak-maahn 百萬

mind, brain nóuh/lóuh 腦

mind, to be displeased gaaiyi
介意

mineral water kwongchyùhn-
sēui 礦泉水

mini màih'néih/léih 迷你

minor (not important) chiyiu ge
次要嘅

minus gáam 減

minute fān (jūng) 分（鐘）

mirror geng 鏡

misfortune m̀h'hóuchói 唔好
彩

Miss síujē 小姐

miss, to (bus, flight etc.) jáu-jó
(bāsí, fēigēi) 走咗（巴士，飛
機）

miss, to (loved one) gwa-jyuh
掛住

missing (absent) kyutjihk 缺席

missing (lost person) sātjūng
失踪

mist bohkmouh 薄霧

mistake cho'ngh 錯誤

mistaken gáau-cho 搞錯

misunderstanding nghwuih 誤
會

mix, to gáau-wàhn 搞勻

mobile phone sáutàih-dihnwá*
手提電話

modern yihndoih 現代

modest, simple poksou 樸素

moment (in a moment) dáng
yātjahn 等一陣

Monday Sīngkèih-yāt/Láihbaai-
yāt 星期一／禮拜一

money chín* 錢

monitor (of computer) hínsih-
hei 顯示器

monkey máhlāu 馬騮

month yuht 月

monument gei'nihm/lihm-bēi
紀念碑

moon yuhtleuhng 月亮

more (comparative) dō-dī 多啲

more of (things) geng-dō 更多

more or less daaih'kói*/koi 大
概

moreover yìhché 而且

morning jīujóu 朝早

mosque Wùihgaau-míu* 回教
廟

mosquito mān 蚊

most (superlative) jeui 最

most (the most of) jeuidō 最多

mostly daaih-bouhfahn 大部分

moth ngòh/òh 蛾

mother màhmā 媽媽

mother-in-law ngoih/oih'móu*,
ngohk/ohk'móu* 外母／岳母

motor, engine mōdá 摩打

motorcycle dihn-dāanchē 電單
車

motor vehicle sīgā-chē 私家車

mountain sāan 山

mouse (animal) lóuhsyú 老鼠

mouse (computer) waaht'syú
滑鼠

moustache wùhsōu 鬍鬚

mouth jéui 嘴

move, to (house) būn'ngūk/ūk
搬屋

move from one place to another
būn 搬

movement, motion duhngjok/
hàhngdung 動作／行動

movie dihnyíng 電影

movie house heiyún* 戲院

Mr sīnsāang 先生

Mrs taaitáai* 太太

MSG meihjīng 味精

much, many dō 多

mud nàih/làih 泥

muscle gēiyuhk 肌肉

music yām'ngohk/ohk 音樂

musical instrument ngohk/ohk'hei 樂器

museum bokmaht-gwún 博物館

mushrooms mòhgū 蘑菇

Muslim (in general) Wùihgaau ge 回教嘅

Muslim (people) Wùihgaautòuh 回教徒

must yātdihng 一定

mutton yèuhngyuhk 羊肉

my, mine ngóh/óh'ge 我嘅

myth sàhnwá* 神話

N

nail (finger, toe) jígaap 指甲

nail (spike) dēng 釘

naked lótái 裸體

name méng* 名

narrow jaak 窄

nation, country gwokgā 國家

national chyùhn'gwok-sing 全國性

nationality gwokjihk 國籍

natural jihyìhn ge 自然嘅

nature daaih-jihyìhn 大自然

naughty wàahnpèih 頑皮

nearby fuhgahn 附近

nearly gēifùh 幾乎

neat, orderly jíngchàih 整齊

necessary bītsēui 必需

neck géng 頸

necklace génglín 頸鏈

necktie lēhngtāai 領呔

need, to need sēuiyiu 需要

needle jām 針

neglect, to fātleuhk 忽略

neighbor lèuhn'gēui 鄰居

neither léuhng go dōu m̀h'haih 兩個都唔係

neither ... nor ... m̀h'haih ... yauh m̀h'haih 唔係 ... 又唔係

nephew (brother's son) jaht 侄

nephew (son of father's sisters/mother's siblings) ngoih/oih'sāng 外甥

nest jeukchàauh 雀巢

net mōhng 網

network gwāanhaih-mōhng 關系網

never wíhngmóuh 永冇

never mind! m̀h'gányiu 唔緊要

nevertheless bātgwo 不過

new sān 新

news sānmán*/sānmàhn 新聞

newspaper boují 報紙

New Zealand Sānsāilàahn 新西蘭

New Zealander Sānsāilàahn-yàhn 新西蘭人

next (in line, sequence) hah yāt go 下一個

next to pòhngbīn 旁邊

next week hah (go) sīngkèih/láihbaai 下 (個) 星期／禮拜

next year mìhng/chēut'nín*/lín* 明年／出年

nice hóu 好

niece (brothers' daughter) jaht'néui*/léui* 侄女

niece (daughter of father's sisters) ngoih/oih'sāng'néui*/léui* 外甥女

niece (daughter of mother's siblings) ngoih/oih'sāng'néui*/léui* 外甥女

night yehmáahn(hāk) 夜晚 (黑)

nightclothes, nightdress seuihyī 睡衣

nightly múihmáahn 每晚

nine gáu 九

nineteen sahp-gáu 十九

ninety gáu-sahp 九十

no, not (with nouns) móuh 冇

no, not (with verbs and adjectives) m̀h'haih 唔係

nobody móuhyàhn 冇人

noise sēng/jaahpsēng 聲 / 雜聲

noisy chòuh 嘈

nonsense faiwá* 廢話

noodles mihn 麵

noon jūngngh 中午

nor yihk m̀h'haih 亦唔係

normal jingsèuhng 正常

north bākbihn 北邊

north-east dūngbāk 東北

north-west sāibāk 西北

nose beihgō 鼻哥

nostril beihgō-lūng 鼻哥窿

not m̀h 唔

not able to understand (by hearing) tēng-m̀h'mìhng 聽唔明

not able to understand (by reading) tái-m̀h'mìhng 睇唔明

not only ... but also bātdaahn ... yìhchē 不但 ... 而且

not yet juhng meih 仲未

note (currency) ngàhn/àhn'jí 銀紙

note (written) jihtìuh 字條

notebook bātgei-bóu 筆記簿

note down, to gei-dāi 記低

nothing móuhyéh 冇嘢

notice tūngjī 通知

notice, to jyuyi 注意

novel síusyut 小説

November Sahp-yāt-yuht 十一月

now yīgā/yìh'gā 依家 / 而家

nowadays yihnsìh 現時

nowhere bíndouh dōu m̀h'hái 邊度都唔喺

nude lótái 裸體

numb màh'muhk 麻木

number houhmáh 號碼

nylon nèih/lèih'lùhng 尼龍

O

o'clock dím(jūng) 點 (鐘)

obedient tēngwah 聽話

obey, to fuhkchùhng 服從

object, thing yéh 嘢

object, to protest fáandeui 反對

occasionally ngáuh/áuh'yìhn'gāan 偶然間

occupation jīkyihp 職業

ocean hóiyèuhng 海洋

October Sahp-yuht 十月

odor, bad smell chauhei 臭氣

of, from (suhkyū) ... ge (屬於) ... 嘅

of course dōngyìhn 當然

off (gone bad) waaih-jó 壞咗

off (turned off) sāan-jó 閂咗

off: to turn something off sāan 閂

offend dākjeuih 得罪

offer, suggest tàihyíh 提議

offering tàihgūng 提供

office séjih-làuh/baahn'gūng-sāt 寫字樓 / 辦公室

official, formal jingsīk ge 正式嘅

officials (government) gūngmouh-yùhn 公務員

often gīngsèuhng 經常

oil yàuh 油

okay dāk 得

old (of persons) lóuh 老

old (of things) gauh 舊

olden times, in gauhsìh 舊時

Olympics Ngou/Ou'wahn-wúi* 奧運會

on, at hái/hèung 喺 / 響

on (turned on) hōi-jó 開咗

on: to turn something on hōi 開

on fire fójūk 火燭

on foot hàahnglouh-heui 行路去

on the way làih-gán 嚟緊

on the whole daaihji-seuhng 大致上

on time jéunsìh 準時

once yāt chi 一次

one yāt 一

one-way ticket dāanchìhng-piu 單程票

one who, the one which ... gó júng yàhn ... 嗰種人

onion yèuhngchūng 洋蔥

only jihnghaih 淨係

open hōi 開

open, to dá-hōi 打開

operating system (computer) chōujok-haihtúng 操作系統

opinion yigin 意見

opponent deuisáu 對手

opportunity geiwuih 機會

oppose, to fáandeui 反對

opposed, in opposition deuilaahp ge 對立嘅

opposite (contrary) sēungfáan 相反

opposite (facing) deuimihn 對面

optional fēi kéuhngjai-sing ge 非強制嘅

or waahkjé 或者

orange (color) cháangsīk 橙色

orange, citrus cháang 橙

order (command) to order mihnglihng 命令

order (placed for food) dím-choi 點菜

order (placed for goods) dehngdāan 訂單

order, sequence chijeuih 次序

orderly, organized yáuh-dihtjeuih-gám* 有秩序咁

organize, arrange ngōn/ōn'pàaih 安排

origin héiyùhn 起源

original jeuichō 最初

originate, come from lòihyùhn yū 來源於

ornament jōngsīk-bán 裝飾品

other kèihtā 其他

other (alternative) lihng'ngoih/oih 另外

ought to yīnggōi 應該

our ngóh/óh'dcih gc 我哋嘅

out chēut-jó-gāai 出咗街

outside ngoih/oih'mihn 外面

outside of hái/héung ... ngoih/oih'mihn 喺/響 ... 外面

oval (shape) tóh'yùhn-yìhng 橢圓形

oven guhklòuh 焗爐

over, finished yùhn-jó 完咗

over: to turn over fāan-gwoheui 翻過去

overcast, cloudy yāmtīn 陰天

overcome, to hākfuhk 克服

overseas hói'ngoih/oih 海外

over there gó'bīn/bihn 嗰邊

overturned fāan-jó 翻咗

owe, to him 欠

own, to yúngyáuh 擁有

own, personal jihgéi ge 自己嘅

own, on one's gūduhk 孤獨

oyster hòuh 蠔

pack, to bāaujōng 包裝

package bāaujōng 包裝

page yihp 頁

paid bēi-jó-chín* 俾咗錢

pain, painful tung 痛

paint yáu* 油

paint, to (a painting) waahk'wá* 畫畫

paint, to (building) yàuh-yáu* 油油

painting wá* 畫

pair of, a yāt deui 一對

pajamas seuihyī 睡衣

palace gūngdihn 宮殿

pan wohk 鑊

panorama chyùhn'gíng 全景

panties tipsān-dyúnfu 貼身短褲

pants fu 褲

paper jí 紙

parcel bāaugwó 包裹

pardon me? what did you say? mē wá* 咩話

parents fuhmóuh 父母

park gūngyún* 公園

park, to (car) paakchē 泊車

part (not whole) bouhfahn 部分

part (of machine) lìhnggín* 零件

participate, to chāamgā 參加

particularly, especially yàuhkèih-sih 尤其是

partly yāt bouhfahn 一部份

partner (in business) paakdong 拍檔

partner (spouse) buhnléuih 伴侶

party (event) lyùhnfūn-wúi* 聯歡會

party (political) jingdóng 政黨

pass, go past gīnggwo 經過

pass, to (exam) hahpgaak 合格

passenger sìhnghaak 乘客

passport wuhjiu 護照

past: go past yuhtgwo 越過

past, former gwoheui 過去

pastime sīuhín 消遣

patient (calm) noih/loih'sām 耐心

patient (doctor's) behngyàhn 病人

pattern, design sīkyéung* 式樣

patterned fóngjouh 彷造

pay, to béi-chín* 俾錢

pay attention làuhyi/jyuyi 留意 / 注意

payment fuhfún 付款

peaceful nìhng/lìhng'jihng 寧靜

peach tóu* 桃

peak, summit sāandéng* 山頂

peanut fāsāng 花生

pear léi 梨

pearl jānjyū 珍珠

pin daaihtàuh-jām 大頭針

pink fánhùhng-sīk 粉紅色

peas chēngdáu* 青豆

peel, to mōkpèih 剝皮

pen mahkséui-bāt 墨水筆

pencil yùhnbāt 鉛筆

penis yāmging 陰莖

people yàhn 人

pepper (black) hāk-wùhjīufán 黑胡椒粉

pepper (chilli) laahtjīu 辣椒

percent baakfahnjī ... 百分之 ...

percentage baakfahn-léut* 百分率

performance yínchēut 演出

perfume hēungséui 香水

perhaps waahkjé 或者

perhaps, probably hó'nàhng/làhng 可能

period (end of a sentence) gitchūk 結束

period (menstrual) yuhtgīng-kèih 月經期

period (of time) sìhkèih 時期

permanent wìhnggáu ge 永久嘅

permit héuihó-jing 許可証

permit, to allow jéunhéui 準許

person yàhn 人

personality singgaak 性格

perspire, to chēuthohn 出汗

pet animal chúngmaht 寵物

petrol dihnyàuh 電油

petrol station dihnyàuh-jaahm 電油站

pharmacy, drugstore yeuhkfòhng 藥房

Philippines Fēileuhtbān 菲律賓

photocopy, to photocopy fūkyan 複印

photograph séung* 相

photograph, to yíngséung* 影相

pick, choose gáan 揀

pick up, to (someone) jip 接

pick up, lift (something) jāp-héi 執起

pickpocket pàhsáu/síutāu 扒手 / 小偷

pickpocket, to pàh 扒

picture　wā*　畫

piece, portion, section　seuipín*　碎片

piece, item　gihn　件

pierce, penetrate　chyūn　穿

pig　jyū　豬

pills　yeuhk'yún　藥丸

pillow　jámtàuh　枕頭

pineapple　bōlò　菠蘿

pink　fánhùhng-sīk　粉紅色

pitcher, jug　séuijūk　水 JUG

pity　hólìhn　可憐

pity: what a pity!　hósīk　可惜

place　deihfōng　地方

place, put　fong　放

plain (level ground)　pìhngyùhn/pìhngdeih　平原 / 平地

plain (not fancy)　poksou　樸素

plan　gaiwaahk　計劃

plan, to　dásyun　打算

plane　fēigēi　飛機

plant　jihkmaht　植物

plant, to　jung　種

plastic　sokgāau　塑膠

plate　dihp　碟

play, to　wáan　玩

play around　jēuikàuh héungsauh　追求享受

plead, to　bihnwuh　辯護

pleasant　lìhng yàhn yuhfaai ge　令人愉快嘅

please go ahead, please　chíng　請

pleased　gōuhing　高興

plug (bath)　sāk　塞

plug (electric)　chaap'táu*/tàuh　插頭

plum　boulām　布冧

plus　gāséuhng　加上

pocket　dói*　袋

point (in time)　sìhhāk　時刻

point, dot　jīmdyūn　尖端

point out　jíchēut　指出

poison　duhkyeuhk　毒藥

poisonous　yáuhduhk ge　有毒嘅

police　gíngchaat-gúk*　警察局

police officer　gíngchaat　警察

polish, to　chaat-gwōng　擦光

politics　jingjih　政治

polite　yáuh-láihmaauh　有禮貌

poor (not rich)　kùhng　窮

popular　làuhhàhng　流行

population　yàhnháu　人口

pork　jyūyuhk　豬肉

port　hóigóng　海港

portion, serve　yāt fahn　一份

possess, to　jimyáuh　佔有

possessions　chòihmaht　財物

possible, possibly　hó'nàhng/làhng　可能

post, column　chyúh　柱

post, mail　gei　寄

postcard　mìhngseun-pín*　明信片

post office　yàuhgúk*　郵局

postpone, to　yìhnkèih　延期

pot　wùh　壺

poultry　gākàhm　家禽

pour, to　dóu　倒

power　lihkleuhng　力量

powerful　kèuhngdaaih　強大

practice, to practice　lihnjaahp　練習

praise　chīngjaan　稱讚

praise, to　jaan　讚

prawn　hā　蝦

prayer, to pray　kèihtóu　祈禱

prefer, to　jūngyi　鐘意

pregnant　wàaihyahn　懷孕

prepare, make ready　jéunbeih　準備

prepared, ready　jéunbeih-hóu　準備好

prescription　yeuhkdāan　藥單

present (gift)　láihmaht　禮物

present (here)　yìh'gā　而家

present, to　gaaisiuh　介紹

presently, nowadays　gahnlòih　近來

present moment, at the　muhkchìhn　目前

president　júngtúng　總統

press, journalism　sānmàhn-gaai　新聞界

P

press, to gīnchìh yīukàuh 堅持要求

pressure ngaak/aak'lihk 壓力

pretend, to jadai 咋帝

pretty leng 靚

prevent, to jójí 阻止

price gachìhn 價錢

pride jihhòuh , jihjyūn-sām 自豪, 自專心

priest sàhnfuh/muhksī 神父 / 牧師

prime minister jūngléih 總理

print, to (from computer) dáyan 打印

prison gāamyuhk 監獄

private sīyàhn 私人

probably daaihkoi 大概

problem mahntàih 問題

produce, to sāngcháan 生產

profession jīkyihp 職業

profit leihyeuhn 利潤

program, schedule jitmuhk 節目

promise, to daapying 答應

pronounce, to faatyām 發音

proof jinggeui 証據

property chòihcháan 財產

protest, to kongyíh 抗議

proud gīu'ngouh/ouh 驕傲

prove, to jingmìhng 証明

public gūngguhng 公共

publish, to chēutbáan 出版

pull, to lāai 拉

pump bāng 泵

punctual jéunsìh 準時

pupil hohksāang 學生

pure sèuhn 純

purple jísīk 紫色

purpose muhkdīk 目的

purse (for money) ngàhn/àhn'bāau 銀包

pursue jēuikàuh 追求

push, to tēui 推

put, place fong 放

put off, delay tēuichìh 推遲

put on (clothes) jeuk 著

puzzled beih màihwaahk 被迷惑

pyjamas seuihyī 睡衣

Q

qualification jīgaak 資格

quarter seifahnjī-yāt 四分之一

queen néuih/léuih'wòhng 女王

question mahntàih 問題

queue, line chèuhnglùhng 長龍

queue, to line up pàaih-déui* 排隊

quick faai 快

quickly hóufaai-gám 好快咁

quiet ngōn/ōn'jihng 安靜

quite (fairly) sēungdōng 相當

quite (very) dīkkok 的確

R

radio sāuyām-gēi 收音機

rail: by rail chóh-fóchē 坐火車

railroad, railway titlouh 鐵路

rain yúh 雨

rain, to lohk-yúh 落雨

raise, lift tàihgōu 提高

raise, to (children) fúyéuhng 撫養

RAM (computer) noih/loih'chyùhn 內存

rank, station in life deihwaih 地位

ranking pàaihmìhng 排名

rare (scarce) hónyáuh ge 罕有嘅

rare (uncooked) bunsāangsuhk 半生熟

rarely, seldom nàahn/làahn'dāk 難得

rat lóuhsyú 老鼠

rate, tariff sāufai 收費

rate of exchange deuiwuhn-léut* 兌換率

rather, fairly béigaau 比較

rather than nìhng/lìhng'hó 寧可

raw, uncooked, rare sāang ge 生嘅

reach, get to daahtdou 達到

react to héi fáanying 起反應

reaction, response fáanying 反應

read, to tái-syū 睇書

ready yihnsìhng 現成

ready, to get jéunbeih 準備

ready, to make jéunbeih-hóu 準備好

realize, be aware of líuhgáai 瞭解

really (in fact) jān ge 真嘅

really (very) fēisèuhng 非常

really? haih mē? 係咩?

rear, tail hauhmihn 後面

reason yùhnyān 原因

reasonable (price) gūngdouh 公道

reasonable (sensible) hahpchìhng-hahpléih 合情合理

receipt sāugeui 收據

receive, to sāu-dóu* 收到

recipe sihkpóu 食譜

recognize, to yihngdāk 認得

recommend, to tēuijin 推薦

recover (cured) hōngfuhk 康復

rectangle chèuhngfōng-yìhng 長方形

red hùhngsīk 紅色

reduce, to gáam-ga 減價

reduction gáamsíu 減少

reflect, to fáanyíng 反映

refrigerator syut'gwaih 雪櫃

refusal, to refuse kéuihjhyuht 拒絕

regarding yáuh'gwāan 有關

region deihkēui 地區

register, to gwahouh 掛號

registered post gwahouh-seun 掛號信

regret, to gám-dou wàihhahm 感到遺憾

regrettably wàihhahm-gám* 遺憾嘅

regular, normal dihngkèih 定期

relatives, family chānchīk 親戚

relax, to fongsūng 放鬆

release, to sīkfong 釋放

religion jūnggaau 宗教

remainder, leftover jihng-lohklàih ge 剩落嚟嘅

remains (historical) gújīk 古蹟

remember, to geidāk 記得

remind, to tàihséng 提醒

rent, to jōu 租

repair, to sāuléih 修理

repeat, to chùhngfūk 重複

replace, to doihtai 代替

reply, response daapfūk 答覆

reply, to (in speech) wùihdaap 回答

reply, to (in writing) wùihfūk 回覆

report bougou 報告

report, to wuihbou 匯報

reporter geijé 記者

request, to (formally) yīukàuh 要求

request, to (informally) chíngkàuh 請求

rescue, to chéunggau 搶救

research, to research yìhn'gau 研究

resemble sēungchíh 相似

reservation (seats) dehngwái* 訂位

reserve (for animals) bóuwuh-kēui 保護區

reserve, to (ask for in advance) yuhdehng 預訂

resident, inhabitant gēuimàhn 居民

resolve, to (a problem) gáaikyut 解決

respect jyūnjuhng 尊重

respect, to jyun'ging 尊敬

R

respond, react fáanying 反應

response, reaction daapfūk 答覆

responsibility jaakyahm 責任

responsible, to be fuhjaak 負責

rest, remainder jihnglohk ge 剩落嘅

rest, to relax yāusīk 休息

restaurant chāan'gwún 餐館

restrain, to yīkjai 抑制

restroom sáisáu-gāan 洗手間

result sìhngjīk 成績

resulting from, as a result gitgwó 結果

resume fūifuhk 恢復

retired teuiyāu 退休

return, to give back wàahn 還

return, to go back fāan-jyuntàuh 返轉頭

return home, to fāan-ngūk/ūk'kéi* 返屋企

return ticket lòihwùih-piu 來回票

reveal, to (make known) kitfaat 揭發

reveal, to (make visible) chìhngyihn 呈現

reverse, to go back diuhtàuh 掉頭

ribbon sīdáai* 絲帶

rice (cooked) baahkfaahn 白飯

rice (plant) douhmáih 稻米

rice (uncooked grains) máih 米

rice fields douhtìhn 稻田

rich fuyuh 富裕

rid: get rid of báai'tyut 擺脱

ride (in car) chòh-chē 坐車

ride, to (bicycle) cháai-dāanchē 踩單車

ride, to (horse) kèhmáh 騎馬

ride, to (motorcycle) jā-dihndāanchē 揸電單車

ride, to (ship) chòh-syùhn 坐船

right, correct jingkok 正確

right-hand side yauh'bīn/bihn 右邊

right now laahphāk/máhseuhng 立刻 / 馬上

rights kyùhnleih 權利

ring (jewelry) gaaijí 戒指

ring, to (on the telephone) dá-dihnwá* 打電話

ring, to (bell) gahm-jūng 撳鐘

rip open, to sī-hōi 撕開

ripe suhk ge 熟嘅

rise, ascend seuhngsīng 上升

rise, increase jānggā 增加

rival deuisáu 對手

river hòh 河

road louh 路

roast, grill sīuhāau 燒烤

rock sehktàuh 石頭

role goksīk 角色

roof ngūk/ūk'déng* 屋頂

room fóng* 房

room, space hūnggāan 空間

root (of plant) gān 根

rope síng 繩

rotten fuhlaahn 腐爛

rough chōulóuh 粗魯

roughly, approximately daaih'yéuk*/yeuk 大約

round (shape) yùhnyìhng 圓形

round, around wàahnyíu 環繞

rubber (eraser) chaatjí-gāau 擦紙膠

rubber (material) jeuhnggāau 橡膠

rude móuh-láihmaauh 冇禮貌

rules kwāijāk 規則

run, to jáu 走

run away jáulóu* 走佬

S

sacred sàhnsing 神聖

sacrifice jaibán 祭品

sacrifice, to hēisāng 犧牲

sad nàahn/làahn'gwo 難過

safe ngōn/ōn'chyùhn 安全

sail, to hōisyùhn/hòhnghàhng 開船 / 航行

salary sānsēui 薪水

sale, for chēutsauh 出售

sale (reduced prices) daaih-gáamga 大減價

sales assistant sauhfo-yùhn 售貨員

salt yìhm 鹽

salty hàahm 鹹

same yātyeuhng 一樣

sample yeuhngbún 樣本

sand sā 沙

sandals lèuhng'hàaih 涼鞋

satisfied múhnyi ge 滿意嘅

satisfied, to satisfy múhnjūk 滿足

Saturday Sīngkèih-luhk/Làihbaai-luhk 星期六 / 禮拜六

sauce jāp 汁

sauce (chilli) laahtjīu-jeung 辣椒醬

save, keep bóu'chyùhn 保存

say, to góng 講

say goodbye douhbiht 道別

say hello mahnhauh 問候

say sorry douhhip 道歉

say thank you douhjeh 道謝

scales ching/tīnpìhng 秤 / 天平

scarce kyutfaht 缺乏

scared pa 怕

scenery jihyìhn fūnggíng 自然風景

schedule sìhgaan-bíu yahtchìhng-bíu 時間表 / 日程表

school hohkhaauh 學校

school child síuhohksāang 小學生

science fōhohk 科學

scissors gaaujín 較剪

Scotland Sōugaaklàahn 蘇格蘭

Scottish (in general) Sōugaaklàahn ge 蘇格蘭嘅

Scottish, Scots Sōugaaklàahn-yàhn 蘇格蘭人

screen (of computer) pìhngmohk 屏幕

screw-driver lòhsīpāi 螺絲批

scrub, to chaat gōnjehng 擦乾淨

sculpture, to sculpt dīusok 雕塑

sea hói 海

seafood hóisīn 海鮮

search for, to wáhn 搵

season gwaijit 季節

seat johwái* 座位

second (in sequence) daihyih 第二

second (instant) míuh 秒

secondary school child jūnghohksāang 中學生

secret beimaht 秘密

secret, to keep a bóumaht 保密

secretary beisyū 秘書

secure, safe ngōn/ōn'chyùhn 安全

see, to tái-gin 睇見

seed júngjí 種子

seek, to chàhmkàuh 尋求

seem, to chíhfùh 似乎

see you later! yātjahn gin 一陣見

seldom hóusíu 好少

select, to tīusyún 挑選

self jihgéi 自己

self-respect/self-esteem jihjyūn-sām 自尊心

sell, to maaih 賣

send, to sung 送

sensible hahp-chìhngléih / mìhngji 合情理 / 明智

sentence geui 句

separate (couple, lovers) fānsáu 分手

separate, to fān-hōi 分開

September Gáu-yuht 九月

sequence, order chijeuih 次序

serious (not funny) yìhmsūk 嚴肅

serious (severe) yìhmjuhng 嚴重

servant gūngyàhn 工人

serve, to waih ... fuhkmouh 為 ... 服務

service fuhkmouh 服務

sesame oil màhyàuh 麻油

sesame seeds jī'màh 芝麻

set tou 套

seven chāt 七

seventeen sahp-chāt 十七

seventy chāt-sahp 七十

several géi (go) 幾（個）

severe yìhmlaih 嚴厲

sew, to fùhngyahn 縫紉

sex, gender singbiht 性別

sex, sexual activity jouh'ngoi/oi 做愛

shack màauhlìuh 茅寮

shade yāmlèuhng deihfōng 陰涼地方

shadow yíng 影

shake, to yìuh 搖

shake something, to yìuhfōng 搖晃

shall, will jēungwúih 將會

shallow chín 淺

shame, disgrace cháu/sāugā 醜／羞家

shame: what a shame! jānhaih hósīk la! 真係可惜喇！

shampoo sáitàuh-séui 洗頭水

Shanghai Seuhnghói 上海

shape yìhngjohng 形狀

shape, to form sìhngyìhng 成形

shark sāyùh 鯊魚

sharp fūngleih 鋒利

shave, to tai-sōu 剃鬚

she, her kéuih 佢

sheet (for bed) chòhngdāan 床單

sheet (of paper) jí 紙

sheep yèuhng 羊

Shinto Sàhndouh 神道

shiny faatgwōng ge 發光嘅

ship syùhn 船

shirt sēutsāam 恤衫

shit sí 屎

shiver, to dá-láahngjan 打冷震

shoes hàaih 鞋

shoot, to (with a gun) hōi-chēung 開槍

shop, store poutáu* 舖頭

shop, go shopping máaih-yéh 買嘢

shopkeeper lóuhbáan 老闆

short (concise) dyún 短

short (not tall) ngái/ái 矮

shorts (short trousers) dyúnfu 短褲

shorts (underpants) dáifu 底褲

short time, a moment dyúnjaahm 短暫

shoulder boktàuh 膊頭

shout, to daaihsēng ngaai/aai 大聲嗌

show (live performance) bíuyín 表演

show, to bēi yàhn tái 俾人睇

shower (for washing) fāsá 花灑

shower (of rain) jaauh'yúh 驟雨

shower, to take a chūng-fāsá 冲花灑

shrimp, prawn saihā 細蝦

shut sāan 閂

shut, to sāan-màaih 閂埋

sibling hīngdaih-jímuih 兄弟姊妹

sick, ill behng-jó 病咗

sick to be (vomit) ngáu/áu'tou 嘔吐

side pòhngbīn 旁邊

sightseeing tái-fūnggíng 睇風景

sign, road louhpáai* 路牌

sign, symbol bīuji 標志

signature, to sign chīm-méng* 簽名

signboard jīupàaih 招牌

silent jihng 靜

silk sīchàuh 絲綢

silver ngàhn/àhn 銀

similar sēungchíh 相似

simple (easy) yùhngyih 容易

simple (uncomplicated) gáandāan 簡單

since jihchùhng 自從

sing, to cheung-gō 唱歌

Singapore Sān'gabō 新加坡

Singaporean (in general) Sān'gabō ge 新加坡嘅

Singaporean (people) Sān'gabō-yàhn 新加坡人

single (not married) dāansān 單身

single (only one) yāt go yàhn 一個人

sir (term of address) sīnsāang 先生

sister (older) jèhjē* 姐姐

sister (younger) mùihmúi* 妹妹

sister-in-law (wife of husband's older brother) sóu 嫂

sister-in-law (wife of husband's younger brother) daihfúh 弟婦

sister-in-law (wife of wife's older/younger brother) káhmmóuh 舅母

sister-in-law (wife's sister) yī姨

sit, to chóh 坐

sit down, to chóh-dāi 坐低

situated, to be waihyū 位於

situation, how things are chìhngfong 情況

six luhk 六

sixteen sahp-luhk 十六

sixty luhk-sahp 六十

size daaihsai 大細

skewer chyunsīu 串燒

skilful suhklihn 熟練

skin pèihfū 皮膚

skirt kwàhn 裙

sky tīnhūng 天空

sleep, to fan'gaau 瞓覺

sleepy ngáahn/áahn'fan 眼瞓

slender saichèuhng 細長

slight síuhéui 少許

slightly sáauwàih 稍為

slim mìuhtíuh 苗條

slippers tōhāai* 拖鞋

slope sāanbō 山坡

slow maahn 慢

slowly maahnmáan*déi* 慢慢地

small sai 細

smart chūngmìhng 聰明

smell, bad odor chaumeih 臭味

smell, to màhn 聞

smile, to siu 笑

smoke yīn 煙

smoke, to (tobacco) sihk-yīn 食煙

smooth (of surfaces) pìhng'waaht 平滑

smooth (unproblematic) seuhnleih 順利

smuggle, to (illegal goods) jáausī 走私

snake sèh 蛇

sneeze hātchī 乞嗤

sneeze, to dá-hātchī 打乞嗤

snow syut 雪

snow, to lohk-syut 落雪

snowpeas hòhlāan-dáu* 荷蘭豆

so (degree) gám*yéung* 咁樣

so that yīhji 以致

so, therefore sóyíh 所以

soak, to jamtau 浸透

soap fāan'gáan 番硯

soccer jūkkàuh 足球

socket (electric) chaap'táu*/tàuh 插頭

socks maht 襪

sofa, couch sōfá* 梳化

soft yúhn 軟

soft drink heiséui 汽水

software (computer) yúhn'gín* 軟件

sold maaih-jó 賣咗

soldier sihbīng 士兵

sold out maaih-yùhn 賣完

S

sole, only jí'haih/wàihyāt 只係／唯一

solid gutái 固體

solve, to (a problem) gáai'kyut 解決

some yāt-dī 一啲

somebody, someone yáuhyàhn 有人

something yáuh-dī yéh 有啲嘢

sometimes yáuhsìh 有時

somewhere máuhchyu 某處

son jái 仔

son-in-law nēuih/léuih'sai 女婿

song gō(kūk) 歌（曲）

soon hóufaai 好快

sore, painful tung 痛

sorrow bēi'ngōi/ōi 悲哀

sorry, to feel regretful hauhfui 後悔

sorry! deui'm̀h'jyuh 對唔住

sort, type júngleuih 種類

sort out, deal with gáai'kyut 解決

sound, noise sēngyām 聲音

soup (clear) chīngtōng 清湯

soup (spicy stew) gāng 羹

sour syūn 酸

source lòih'yùhn 來源

south nàahm/làahm'bīn/bihn 南邊

south-east dūng'nàahm/làahm 東南

south-west sāi'nàahm/làahm 西南

souvenir géi'nihm/lihm'bán 紀念品

soy sauce (salty) sāangchāu 生抽

soy sauce (sweet) lóuhchāu 老抽

space hūnggāan/deihfōng 空間／地方

spacious futlohk 闊落

speak, to góng 講

special dahkbiht 特別

spectacles ngáahn/áahn'géng* 眼鏡

speech, to make a speech yín'góng 演講

speed chūkdouh 速度

spell, to chyun 串

spend, to sáichín* 洗錢

spices hēunglíu* 香料

spicy gā hēunglíu* ge 加香料嘅

spinach bōchoi 菠菜

spine buijek-gwāt 背脊骨

spiral lòhsyùhn-yìhng 螺旋形

spirits, hard liquor lihtjáu 烈酒

spoiled (of children) jungwaaih-jó 縱壞咗

spoiled (of food) waaih-jó / sūk-jó 壞咗／叔咗

spoon chìhgāng 匙羹

sponge hóimìhn 海棉

sports wahnduhng 運動

spotted (pattern) bāandím ge 斑點嘅

spray panmouh-hei 噴霧器

spring (metal part) daahn'gūng 彈弓

spring (of water) kwongchyùhn-séui 礦泉水

spring (season) chēuntīn 春天

spouse pui'ngáuh/áuh 配偶

square (shape) jingfōng-yìhng 正方形

square, town square gwóngchèuhng 廣場

squid yàuhyú* 鱿魚

staff gūngjok yàhn'yùhn 工作人員

stain wūdím 污點

stairs làuhtāi 樓梯

stall (of vendor) tāan 攤

stall, to (car) séifó 死火

stamp (ink) goijēung 蓋章

stamp (postage) yàuhpiu 郵票

stand, to kéih 企

stand up, to kéih-héisān 企起身

star sīng 星

start, beginning hōichí 開始
start, to faatduhng 發動
stationery màhn'geuih 文具
statue yàhnjeuhng 人像
stay, remain làuhdāi 留低
stay overnight, to gwo-yē*/yeh 過夜
steal, to tāu 偷
steam jīnghei 蒸汽
steamed jīng ge 蒸嘅
steel gong 鋼
steer, to gasái 駕駛
step bouh 步
steps, stairs làuhtāi-kāp 樓梯級
stick, pole gwan 棍
stick out, to gīnchìh-dou dái 堅持到底
stick to, to jūngyū 忠於
sticky chī-nahp/lahp-nahp/lahp 黐笠笠
sticky rice noh/loh'máih 糯米
stiff ngaahng/aahng 硬
still, quiet pìhngjihng 平靜
still, even now yìhngyìhn 仍然
stingy gūhòhn 孤寒
stink, to faatchau 發臭
stomach, belly tóuh 肚
stone sehktàuh 石頭
stool dang 凳
stop (bus, train) jaahm 站
stop, to tìhng 停
stop by, to pay a visit seuhnlouh baaifóng 順路拜訪
stop it! m̀h'hóu joi gám*yéung* 唔好再咁樣
store, shop poutáu* 舖頭
store, to chyúhchòhng 儲藏
storm dáfūng 打風
story (of a building) chàhng/láu* 層 / 樓
story (tale) gú*jái 故仔
stout gitsaht 結實
stove, cooker lòuhtàuh 爐頭
straight (not crooked) jihk 直
straight ahead yātjihkheui 一直去

strait hóihahp 海峽
strange kèihgwaai 奇怪
stranger sāangbóu-yàhn 生埠人
street gāai 街
strength lihk 力
strict yìhmgaak 嚴格
strike, to go on bah-gūng 罷工
strike, hit dá 打
string síng 繩
striped gaantíu* ge 間條嘅
strong jong 壯
stubborn, determined wàahn'gu 頑固
stuck, won't move gihp-jyuh 夾住
student hohksāang 學生
study, learn hohk 學
stupid bahn/chéun 笨 / 蠢
style fūnggaak 風格
succeed, to (follow) gaisìhng 繼承
success sìhnggūng 成功
such gám*yéung* 咁樣
such as, for example laihyùh 例如
suck, to kāp 吸
suddenly dahkyìhn 突然
suffer, to sauhfú 受苦
suffering tungfú 痛苦
sugar tòhng 糖
sugarcane je 蔗
suggestion, to suggest tàihyíh 提議
suit, business sāijōng 西裝
suitable, fitting ngāam/āam'sān 啱身
suitcase pèihgīp* 皮夾
summer hahtīn 夏天
summit, peak sāanténg* 山頂
sun taaiyèuhng 太陽
Sunday Sīngkèih-yaht/Láihbaai-yaht 星期日 / 禮拜日
sunlight yèuhnggwōng 陽光
sunscreen lotion taaiyèuhng-yàuh/fòhngsaai-yàuh 太陽油 / 防晒油

sunny chìhnglóhng 晴朗
sunrise yahtchēut 日出
sunset yahtlohk 日落
supermarket chīukāp-
  sìhchèuhng 超級市場
suppose, to gádihng 假定
sure hángdihng/kokdihng 肯
  定 / 確定
surf, to chūng-lohng 冲浪
surfing on the Internet sēuhng-
  móhng 上網
surface bíumihn 表面
surface mail hói/luhk'yàuh 海
  郵 / 陸郵
surname sing 姓
surprised gīngkèih / gám-dou
  yi'ngoih/oih 驚奇 / 感到意外
surprising lìhng yàhn gám-dou
  yi'ngoih/oih 令人感到意外
surroundings wàahn'gíng 環
  境
survive, to sāngchyùhn 生存
suspect, to wàaihyìh 懷疑
suspicion yìhsām 疑心
swallow, to tān 吞
sweat hohn 汗
sweat, to chēut-hohn 出汗
sweep, to soudeih 掃地
sweet (taste) tìhm 甜
sweet, dessert tìhmbán 甜品
sweet and sour tìhmsyūn 甜
  酸
sweetcorn sūkmáih 粟米
sweets, candy tóng* 糖
swim, to yàuhséui 游水
swimming costume yàuhséui-
  sāam 游水衫
swimming pool yàuhwìhng-
  chìh 游泳池
swing, to yìuhbáai 搖擺
switch jai 掣
switch, to change jyún 轉
switch on, turn on hōi-jai 開掣
switch off, turn off sāan-jó 閂
  咗
synthetic yàhnjouh ge 人造嘅
system haihtúng 系統

T

table tói 檯
tablecloth tóibou 檯布
tablets yeuhk'yún 藥丸
tail mēih 尾
take, to remove ló-jáu 攞走
take care of, to fuhjaak 負責
take off (clothes) tyut 脫
talk, to kīnggái 傾偈
tall gōu 高
tame sèuhn 馴
Taoism Douhgaau 道教
tape, adhesive gāaují 膠紙
tape recording luhkyām 綠音
taste meihdouh 味道
taste, to (sample) si 試
taste, to (salty, spicy) si-meih
  試味
tasty hóusihk 好食
taxi dīksí 的士
tea chàh 茶
teach, to gaau 教
teacher gaausī 教師
team deuih 隊
tear, to rip sī-hōi 撕開
tears ngáahn/áahn'leuih 眼淚
teenager chīngsiu'nìhn/lìhn
  青少年
teeshirt tīsēut T恤
teeth ngàh/àh 牙
telephone dihnwá* 電話
telephone number dihnwá*
  houhmáh 電話號碼
television dihnsih 電視
tell, to (a story) góng 講
tell, to (let know) wah béi ... jī
  話俾 ... 知
temperature (body) táiwān 體
  溫
temperature (heat) wāndouh
  溫度
temple (Chinese) jih'yún 寺院
temporary jaahmsìh 暫時
ten sahp 十
ten million chīn-maahn 千萬
tendon gān 筋

tennis mōhngkàuh 網球

tens of, multiples of ten géi-sahp 幾十

tense gánjēung 緊張

ten thousand maahn 萬

terrible hópa 可怕

test siyihm 試驗

test, to chāakyihm 測驗

testicles gōuyún 睾丸

than béi 比

Thai (in general) Taaigwok ge 泰國嘅

Thai (language) Taaimán*/mâhn 泰文

Thai (people) Taaigwok-yàhn 泰國人

Thailand Taaigwok 泰國

thankyou, to thank m̀h'gōi/dōjeh 唔該 / 多謝

that, those gó , gódī 嗰, 嗰啲

theater (drama) keuhk'yún 劇院

their, theirs kéuihdeih ge 佢哋嘅

then yìhnhauh 然後

there gódouh/gósyu 嗰度 / 嗰處

therefore yānchí 因此

there is, there are yáuh 有

these nī/lī'dī 呢啲

they, them kéuihdeih 佢哋

thick (of liquids) nùhng/lùhng 濃

thick (of things) háuh 厚

thief chāak*/chaahk 賊

thigh daaihtéui 大腿

thin (of liquids) hēi 稀

thin (of persons) sau 瘦

thing yéh 嘢

think, to ponder séung/háauleuih 想 / 考慮

think, to have an opinion yìhngwàih 認為

third (1/3) sāamfahnjī-yāt 三分之一

third (in a series) daihsāam 第三

thirsty háu'hot 口渴

thirty sāam-sahp 三十

this nī/lī 呢

though sēuiyìhn 雖然

thoughts séungfaat/sīséung 想法 / 思想

thousand chīn 千

thread sin 線

threaten, to húnghaak 恐嚇

three sāam 三

throat hàuhlùhng 喉嚨

through, past tūnggwo 通過

throw, to dám 揼

throw away, throw out dám-jó 揼咗

thunder dálèuih 打雷

Thursday Sīngkèih-sei/Láihbaai-sei 星期四 / 禮拜四

thus, so yūsih 於是

ticket fēi 飛

tidy jínggit 整潔

tidy up sāusahp 收拾

tie, necktie léhngtāai 領呔

tie, to bóng 綁

tiger lóuhfú 老虎

tight gán 緊

time sìhgaan 時間

time: from time to time gaanjūng 間中

times (multiplying) sìhng 乘

timetable sìhgaan-bíu 時間表

tiny saisíu 細小

tip (end) jīmdyūn 尖端

tip (gratuity) tīpsí 貼士

tired (sleepy) ngáahn/áahn'fahn 眼瞓

tired (worn out) gwuih 癐

title (of book, film) bīutàih 標題

title (of person) hàahmtàuh 銜頭

to, toward heung/deui 向 / 對

toasted hong 烘

today gāmyaht 今日

toe geukjí 腳趾

tofu dauhfuh 豆腐

together yātchàih 一齊

T

toilet chisó / sáisáu-gāan 廁所 / 洗手間

tomato fāanké 蕃茄

tomorrow tīngyaht 聽日

tongue leih 脷

tonight gāmmáahn 今晚

too (also) dōuhaih 都係

too (excessive) taai 太

too much taai dō 太多

tool gūnggeuih 工具

tooth ngàh/àh 牙

toothbrush ngàh/àh'cháat* 牙刷

toothpaste ngàh/àh'gōu 牙膏

top déng* 頂

topic tàihmuhk 題目

torch, flashlight dihntúng 電筒

total yātguhng 一共

touch, to mō 摸

tourist léuihhaak/yàuhhaak 旅客 / 遊客

toward (people/place) heung 向

towel mòuhgān 毛巾

tower taap 塔

town síhjan 市鎮

toy wuhn'geuih 玩具

trade maauhyihk 貿易

trade, to exchange gāauyihk 交易

traditional chyùhntúng 傳統

traffic gāautūng 交通

train fóchē 火車

train station fóchē-jaahm 火車站

training fanlihn 訓練

translate, to fāanyihk 翻譯

travel, to leuihhàhng 旅行

traveler leuihhaak 旅客

tray tokpún* 托盤

treat (something special) tìhm'táu*/tàuh 甜頭

treat, to (behave towards) deui (yàhn) 對 (人)

treat, to (medically) yī 醫

tree syuh 樹

triangle sāamgok-yìhng 三角形

tribe bouhlohk 部落

trip, journey leuihhàhng/ leuihchìhng 旅行 / 旅程

troops gwāndéui* 軍隊

trouble, troublesome màhfàahn 麻煩

trousers fu 褲

truck fochē 貨車

true jān 真

truly jānsìhng-gám* 真誠咁

trust, to seunyahm 信任

try, to si 試

try on (clothes) sisān 試身

Tuesday Sīngkèih-yih/ Láihbaai-yih 星期二 / 禮拜二

turn around, to jyun 轉

turn off, to sāan/sīk 閂 / 熄

turn on, to hōi 開

turtle (land) wūgwāi 烏龜

turtle (sea) hóigwāi 海龜

TV dihnsih-gēi 電視機

twelve sahp-yih 十二

twenty yih-sahp 二十

twice léuhng chi 兩次

two (measure) léuhng 兩

two (numeral) yih 二

type, sort júngleuih 種類

type, to dájih 打字

typhoon dáfūng 打風

typical dínyìhng 典型

U

ugly cháuyēung* 醜樣

umbrella jē 遮

uncle (father's older brother) baak 伯

uncle (father's younger brother) sūk 叔

uncle (husband of father's sister) gūjéung* 姑丈

uncle (husband of mother's sister) yìhjéung* 姨丈

uncle (mother's brother) káuhfú* 舅父

under hahmihn 下面

undergo, to gīnggwo 經過

underpants dáifu 底褲
undershirt dáisāam 底衫
understand mìhng 明
understood (by hearing) tēng-mìhng 聽明
understood (by reading) tái-mìhng 睇明
underwear dáisāam 底衫
undressed, to get chèuih-sāam 除衫
unfortunately m̀h'hóuchói 唔好彩
unemployed sātyihp 失業
unhappy m̀h'hōisām 唔開心
United Kingdom Yīnggwok 英國
United States Méihgwok 美國
university daaihhohk 大學
unleaded petrol mòuhyùhn-dihnyàuh 無鉛電油
unless chèuihfēi 除非
unlucky dōumùih 倒霉
unnecessary dōyùh ge 多餘嘅
unripe meihsuhk 未熟
until jihkdou 直到
up, upward heungseuhng 向上
upset, unhappy m̀h'hōisām 唔開心
upside down dou'jyun 倒轉
upstairs làuhseuhng 樓上
urban sìhngsìh ge 城市嘅
urge, to push for chēui 催
urgent gán'gāp 緊急
urinate, to síubihn 小便
urine niuh 尿
us ngóh/óh'deih 我哋
use, to yuhng 用
used to jaahpgwaan 習慣
useful yáuhyuhng ge 有用嘅
useless móuhyuhng ge 冇用嘅
usual pìhngsèuhng 平常
usually tūngsèuhng 通常
uterus jígūng 子宮

V

vacation gakèih 假期

vaccination dá-fòhngyihk-jām 打防疫針
vagina yāmdouh 陰道
vague hàhmwùh 含糊
valid yáuhhaauh 有效
valley sāan'gūk 山谷
value (cost) gajihk 價值
value, good jihkdāk 值得
value, to juhngsih 重視
vase fāpìhng 花瓶
VCR luhkyíng-gēi 錄影機
vegetable sōchoi 蔬菜
vegetarian sousihk ge 素食嘅
vehicle chē 車
vertical sèuihjihk 垂直
very, extremely gihk 極
vest, undershirt buisām 背心
via louhgīng 路經
video cassette sipluhk-dáai* 攝錄帶
video recorder sipluhk-gēi 攝錄機
videotape, to sipluhk 攝錄
Vietnam Yuht'nàahm/làahm 越南
Vietnamese (in general) Yuht'nàahm/làahm ge 越南嘅
Vietnamese (language) Yuht'nàahm/làahm-wá* 越南話
Vietnamese (people) Yuht'nàahm/làahm-yàhn 越南人
view, panorama fūnggíng 風景
view, look at tái-fūnggíng 睇風景
village chyūnjōng 村莊
vinegar chou 醋
visa chīmjing 簽証
visit chāamgwūn 參觀
visit, to pay a fóngmahn 訪問
voice sēngyām 聲音
voicemail dihnwá* làuhyìhn 電話留言
volcano fósāan 火山
vomit, to ngáu/áu 嘔
vote, to tàuh-piu 投票

W

wages yàhn'gūng 人工

wait for, to dáng 等

waiter, waitress sihying-sāng 侍應生

wake up séng* 醒

wake someone up giu-séng* 叫醒

Wales Wāiyíhsī 威爾斯

walk, to hàahng 行

walking distance hàahng-dāk-dou 行得到

wall chèuhng 牆

wallet ngàhn/àhn'bāau 銀包

want, to yiu 要

war jinjāng 戰爭

war, to make dá-jeung 打仗

warm, warmth wāanyúhn 温暖

warning, to warn gínggou 警告

wash, to sái 洗

wash the dishes sái-wún 洗碗

watch (wristwatch) sáubīu 手錶

watch, to tái 睇

watch over, guard hōn'gwún 看管

water séui 水

water buffalo séui'ngàuh/àuh 水牛

waterfall buhkbou 瀑布

watermelon sāigwā 西瓜

wave (in sea) bōlohng 波浪

wave, to jīusáu 招手

wax laahp 蠟

way, method fōngfaat 方法

way: by way of louhging 路經

way in yahpháu 入口

way out chēutháu 出口

we, us ngóh/óh'deih 我哋

weak yeuhk 弱

wealthy yáuhchín*/fuyuh 有錢/富裕

weapon móuhhei 武器

wear, to jeuk 著

weary gwuih 癐

weather tīnhei 天氣

weave, to pīnjīk 編織

website móhngjaahm 網站

wedding fānláih 婚禮

Wednesday Sīngkèih-sāam/Láihbaai-sāam 星期三/禮拜三

week sīngkèih/láihbaai 星期

weekend jāumuht 週末

weekly múih go sīngkèih/láihbaai, múih jāu 每個星期/禮拜, 每週

weep, to haam 喊

weigh, to ching/bohng 秤/磅

weigh out, to ching-chēut 秤出

weight chúhngleuhng 重量

weight (body) táichúhng 體重

weight, to gain jāng-bóng* 增磅

weight, to lose gáam-bóng*/gáam-fèih 減磅/減肥

welcome!, welcome, to fūnyìhng 歡迎

well (for water) jéng 井

well (good) hóu 好

well-behaved kwāi'kwāi-géuigéui 規規矩矩

well-cooked, well-done jyú-tau 煮透

well done! jouh-dāk hóu! 做得好

well-mannered yáuh-láihmaauh 有禮貌

well off, wealthy yáuhchín* 有錢/富裕

Welsh (in general) Wāiyíhsī ge 威爾斯嘅

Welsh (people) Wāiyíhsī-yàhn 威爾斯人

west sāi'bīn/bihn 西邊

Westerner Sāifōng-yàhn 西方人

wet sāp 濕

what mātyéh 乜嘢

what for dímgáai 點解

what kind of bīn júng 邊種